18-1 WORK TOGETHER, p. 459

Journalizing and posting purchase on account transactions

4., 5., 6.

PURCHASES JOURNAL   PAGE 4

	DATE		ACCOUNT CREDITED	PURCH. NO.	POST. REF.	PURCHASES DR. ACCTS. PAY. CR.	
1							1
2							2
3							3
4							4
5							5
6							6
7							7
8							8
9							9
10							10
11							11
12							12
13							13
14							14
15							15
16							16
17							17
18							18
19							19
20							20
21							21
22							22
23							23
24							24
25							25
26							26
27							27
28							28
29							29
30							30
31							31
32							32

D1473472

Journalizing and posting purchase on account transactions

7., 8., 9.

PURCHASES JOURNAL   PAGE 3

	DATE		ACCOUNT CREDITED	PURCH. NO.	POST. REF.	PURCHASES DR. ACCTS. PAY. CR.	
1							1
2							2
3							3
4							4
5							5
6							6
7							7
8							8
9							9
10							10
11							11
12							12
13							13
14							14
15							15
16							16
17							17
18							18
19							19
20							20
21							21
22							22
23							23
24							24
25							25
26							26
27							27
28							28
29							29
30							30
31							31
32							32

18-1 WORK TOGETHER (concluded)

6.   **GENERAL LEDGER**

ACCOUNT Accounts Payable   ACCOUNT NO. 2115

DATE		ITEM	POST. REF.	DEBIT	CREDIT	BALANCE	
						DEBIT	CREDIT
20-- Apr.	1	Balance	✔				8 7 6 0 00

ACCOUNT Purchases   ACCOUNT NO. 5105

DATE		ITEM	POST. REF.	DEBIT	CREDIT	BALANCE	
						DEBIT	CREDIT
20-- Apr.	1	Balance	✔			18 7 8 1 00	

5.   **ACCOUNTS PAYABLE LEDGER**

VENDOR Delta Manufacturing   VENDOR NO. 210

DATE		ITEM	POST. REF.	DEBIT	CREDIT	CREDIT BALANCE
20-- Apr.	1	Balance	✔			2 2 4 5 00

VENDOR Farris, Inc.   VENDOR NO. 220

DATE		ITEM	POST. REF.	DEBIT	CREDIT	CREDIT BALANCE
20-- Apr.	1	Balance	✔			1 2 5 7 00

VENDOR Williams Company   VENDOR NO. 230

DATE		ITEM	POST. REF.	DEBIT	CREDIT	CREDIT BALANCE

9. **GENERAL LEDGER**

ACCOUNT Accounts Payable   ACCOUNT NO. 2115

DATE		ITEM	POST. REF.	DEBIT	CREDIT	BALANCE	
						DEBIT	CREDIT
Mar.	1	Balance	✔				3 1 7 6 00

ACCOUNT Purchases   ACCOUNT NO. 5105

DATE		ITEM	POST. REF.	DEBIT	CREDIT	BALANCE	
						DEBIT	CREDIT
Mar.	1	Balance	✔			12 7 1 0 00	

8. **ACCOUNTS PAYABLE LEDGER**

VENDOR Lambert Industries   VENDOR NO. 310

DATE		ITEM	POST. REF.	DEBIT	CREDIT	CREDIT BALANCE
Mar.	1	Balance	✔			1 6 2 00

VENDOR MJK, Inc.   VENDOR NO. 340

DATE		ITEM	POST. REF.	DEBIT	CREDIT	CREDIT BALANCE
Mar.	1	Balance	✔			1 7 1 8 00

VENDOR Taylor Imports   VENDOR NO. 360

DATE		ITEM	POST. REF.	DEBIT	CREDIT	CREDIT BALANCE

18-2 WORK TOGETHER, p. 464

Recording cash payments for expenses and purchases using a cash payments journal

CASH PAYMENTS JOURNAL

PAGE 4

DATE	ACCOUNT TITLE	CK. NO.	POST. REF.	GENERAL DEBIT	GENERAL CREDIT	ACCOUNTS PAYABLE DEBIT	PURCHASES DISCOUNT CREDIT	CASH CREDIT
				1	2	3	4	5
1								
2								
3								
4								
5								
6								
7								
8								
9								
10								
11								
12								
13								
14								
15								
16								
17								
18								
19								
20								
21								
22								
23								
24								

Recording cash payments for expenses and purchases using a cash payments journal

CASH PAYMENTS JOURNAL

PAGE 6

DATE	ACCOUNT TITLE	CK. NO.	POST. REF.	GENERAL DEBIT	GENERAL CREDIT	ACCOUNTS PAYABLE DEBIT	PURCHASES DISCOUNT CREDIT	CASH CREDIT

18-3 **WORK TOGETHER, p. 469**

Journalizing and posting cash payments using a cash payments journal

3., 4.

CASH PAYMENTS JOURNAL

PAGE 5

| | | | | | GENERAL | | ACCOUNTS PAYABLE DEBIT | PURCHASES DISCOUNT CREDIT | CASH CREDIT |
DATE	ACCOUNT TITLE	CK. NO.	POST. REF.	DEBIT	CREDIT			
									1
									2
									3
									4
									5
									6
									7
									8

3.

PETTY CASH REPORT

Date: _____   Custodian: _____

Explanation	Reconciliation	Replenish Amount

**Fund total
Payments:**

Less: Total payments
Equals: Recorded amount on hand
Less: Actual amount on hand
Equals: Cash short (over)
Amount to replenish

Journalizing and posting cash payments using a cash payments journal

5., 6.

CASH PAYMENTS JOURNAL

PAGE 7

					1	2	3	4	5
DATE	ACCOUNT TITLE	CK. NO.	POST. REF.		GENERAL		ACCOUNTS PAYABLE DEBIT	PURCHASES DISCOUNT CREDIT	CASH CREDIT
					DEBIT	CREDIT			
1									
2									
3									
4									
5									
6									
7									
8									

5.

PETTY CASH REPORT

Date: _____   Custodian: _____

Explanation   Reconciliation   Replenish Amount

Fund total
Payments:

Less: Total payments
Equals: Recorded amount on hand
Less: Actual amount on hand
Equals: Cash short (over)
Amount to replenish

18-3 WORK TOGETHER (continued)

4.   **GENERAL LEDGER**

ACCOUNT Cash   ACCOUNT NO. 1105

DATE	ITEM	POST. REF.	DEBIT	CREDIT	BALANCE DEBIT	BALANCE CREDIT
20-- May 1	Balance	✔			9 7 2 1 60	

ACCOUNT Petty Cash   ACCOUNT NO. 1110

DATE	ITEM	POST. REF.	DEBIT	CREDIT	BALANCE DEBIT	BALANCE CREDIT
20-- May 1	Balance	✔			2 0 0 00	

ACCOUNT Supplies   ACCOUNT NO. 1140

DATE	ITEM	POST. REF.	DEBIT	CREDIT	BALANCE DEBIT	BALANCE CREDIT
20-- May 1	Balance	✔			2 4 6 7 30	

ACCOUNT Accounts Payable   ACCOUNT NO. 2115

DATE	ITEM	POST. REF.	DEBIT	CREDIT	BALANCE DEBIT	BALANCE CREDIT
20-- May 1	Balance	✔				9 7 2 4 60

ACCOUNT Advertising Expense   ACCOUNT NO. 6105

DATE	ITEM	POST. REF.	DEBIT	CREDIT	BALANCE DEBIT	BALANCE CREDIT
20-- May 1	Balance	✔			1 4 9 7 60	

4.

GENERAL LEDGER

ACCOUNT Cash Short and Over   ACCOUNT NO. 6110

DATE	ITEM	POST. REF.	DEBIT	CREDIT	BALANCE	
					DEBIT	CREDIT
20-- May 1	Balance	✔			3 10	

ACCOUNT Miscellaneous Expense   ACCOUNT NO. 6135

DATE	ITEM	POST. REF.	DEBIT	CREDIT	BALANCE	
					DEBIT	CREDIT
20-- May 1	Balance	✔			1 29 1 05	

ACCOUNTS PAYABLE LEDGER

VENDOR Wilhelm, Inc.   VENDOR NO. 390

DATE	ITEM	POST. REF.	DEBIT	CREDIT	CREDIT BALANCE
20-- May 1	Balance	✔			3 5 90 00

VENDOR   VENDOR NO.

DATE	ITEM	POST. REF.	DEBIT	CREDIT	CREDIT BALANCE

18-3 ON YOUR OWN (continued)

6.   **GENERAL LEDGER**

ACCOUNT Cash   ACCOUNT NO. 1105

DATE		ITEM	POST. REF.	DEBIT	CREDIT	BALANCE DEBIT	BALANCE CREDIT
20-- July	1	Balance	✔			6 2 8 7 16	

ACCOUNT Petty Cash   ACCOUNT NO. 1110

DATE		ITEM	POST. REF.	DEBIT	CREDIT	BALANCE DEBIT	BALANCE CREDIT
20-- July	1	Balance	✔			2 0 0 00	

ACCOUNT Supplies   ACCOUNT NO. 1140

DATE		ITEM	POST. REF.	DEBIT	CREDIT	BALANCE DEBIT	BALANCE CREDIT
20-- July	1	Balance	✔			2 1 7 9 60	

ACCOUNT Accounts Payable   ACCOUNT NO. 2115

DATE		ITEM	POST. REF.	DEBIT	CREDIT	BALANCE DEBIT	BALANCE CREDIT
20-- July	1	Balance	✔				8 7 9 2 19

ACCOUNT Purchases Discount   ACCOUNT NO. 5110

DATE		ITEM	POST. REF.	DEBIT	CREDIT	BALANCE DEBIT	BALANCE CREDIT
20-- July	1	Balance	✔				1 6 3 2 10

6.

GENERAL LEDGER

ACCOUNT Cash Short and Over   ACCOUNT NO. 6110

DATE		ITEM	POST. REF.	DEBIT	CREDIT	BALANCE	
						DEBIT	CREDIT
20-- July	1	Balance	✔			4 16	

ACCOUNT Miscellaneous Expense   ACCOUNT NO. 6135

DATE		ITEM	POST. REF.	DEBIT	CREDIT	BALANCE	
						DEBIT	CREDIT
20-- July	1	Balance	✔			4 6 1 9 80	

ACCOUNT Repair Expense   ACCOUNT NO. 6150

DATE		ITEM	POST. REF.	DEBIT	CREDIT	BALANCE	
						DEBIT	CREDIT
20-- July	1	Balance	✔			9 1 6 00	

ACCOUNTS PAYABLE LEDGER

VENDOR Caliber Company   VENDOR NO. 220

DATE		ITEM	POST. REF.	DEBIT	CREDIT	CREDIT BALANCE
20-- July	1	Balance	✔			2 7 4 0 00

18-4 WORK TOGETHER, p. 475

Journalizing and posting transactions using a general journal

4., 5.

GENERAL JOURNAL   PAGE 3

	DATE	ACCOUNT TITLE	DOC. NO.	POST. REF.	DEBIT	CREDIT	
1							1
2							2
3							3
4							4
5							5
6							6
7							7
8							8
9							9
10							10
11							11
12							12
13							13
14							14
15							15
16							16
17							17
18							18
19							19
20							20
21							21
22							22
23							23
24							24
25							25
26							26
27							27
28							28
29							29
30							30
31							31
32							32

ON YOUR OWN, p. 475

Journalizing and posting transactions using a general journal

6., 7.

GENERAL JOURNAL

PAGE 5

	DATE	ACCOUNT TITLE	DOC. NO.	POST. REF.	DEBIT	CREDIT	
1							1
2							2
3							3
4							4
5							5
6							6
7							7
8							8
9							9
10							10
11							11
12							12
13							13
14							14
15							15
16							16
17							17
18							18
19							19
20							20
21							21
22							22
23							23
24							24
25							25
26							26
27							27
28							28
29							29
30							30
31							31
32							32

18-4 WORK TOGETHER (continued)

5.   GENERAL LEDGER

ACCOUNT Supplies   ACCOUNT NO. 1140

DATE		ITEM	POST. REF.	DEBIT	CREDIT	BALANCE	
						DEBIT	CREDIT
20-- Mar.	1	Balance	✔			2 7 6 3 00	

ACCOUNT Store Equipment   ACCOUNT NO. 1215

DATE		ITEM	POST. REF.	DEBIT	CREDIT	BALANCE	
						DEBIT	CREDIT
20-- Mar.	1	Balance	✔			12 7 6 1 00	

ACCOUNT Accounts Payable   ACCOUNT NO. 2115

DATE		ITEM	POST. REF.	DEBIT	CREDIT	BALANCE	
						DEBIT	CREDIT
20-- Mar.	1	Balance	✔				3 1 3 1 00

ACCOUNT Purchases Returns and Allowances   ACCOUNT NO. 5115

DATE		ITEM	POST. REF.	DEBIT	CREDIT	BALANCE	
						DEBIT	CREDIT
20-- Mar.	1	Balance	✔				6 9 2 00

ACCOUNT   ACCOUNT NO.

DATE		ITEM	POST. REF.	DEBIT	CREDIT	BALANCE	
						DEBIT	CREDIT

5. **ACCOUNTS PAYABLE LEDGER**

VENDOR Hughes Supply

VENDOR NO. 420

DATE		ITEM	POST. REF.	DEBIT	CREDIT	CREDIT BALANCE
20-- Mar.	1	Balance	✔			4 7 2 00

VENDOR Retail Displays, Inc.

VENDOR NO. 430

DATE		ITEM	POST. REF.	DEBIT	CREDIT	CREDIT BALANCE
20-- Mar.	1	Balance	✔			1 6 8 7 00

VENDOR Trainor Company

VENDOR NO. 450

DATE		ITEM	POST. REF.	DEBIT	CREDIT	CREDIT BALANCE
20-- Mar.	1	Balance	✔			9 7 2 00

VENDOR

VENDOR NO.

DATE	ITEM	POST. REF.	DEBIT	CREDIT	CREDIT BALANCE

VENDOR

VENDOR NO.

DATE	ITEM	POST. REF.	DEBIT	CREDIT	CREDIT BALANCE

18-4 **ON YOUR OWN (continued)**

7.   **GENERAL LEDGER**

ACCOUNT Supplies   ACCOUNT NO. 1140

DATE		ITEM	POST. REF.	DEBIT	CREDIT	BALANCE	
						DEBIT	CREDIT
20-- May	1	Balance	✔			4 6 9 2 00	

ACCOUNT Office Equipment   ACCOUNT NO. 1205

DATE		ITEM	POST. REF.	DEBIT	CREDIT	BALANCE	
						DEBIT	CREDIT
20-- May	1	Balance	✔			16 7 1 8 00	

ACCOUNT Accounts Payable   ACCOUNT NO. 2115

DATE		ITEM	POST. REF.	DEBIT	CREDIT	BALANCE	
						DEBIT	CREDIT
20-- May	1	Balance	✔				2 2 1 3 00

ACCOUNT Purchases Returns and Allowances   ACCOUNT NO. 5115

DATE		ITEM	POST. REF.	DEBIT	CREDIT	BALANCE	
						DEBIT	CREDIT
20-- May	1	Balance	✔				2 7 6 1 00

ACCOUNT   ACCOUNT NO.

DATE		ITEM	POST. REF.	DEBIT	CREDIT	BALANCE	
						DEBIT	CREDIT

7.   **ACCOUNTS PAYABLE LEDGER**

vendor Best Industries   VENDOR NO. 210

DATE		ITEM	POST. REF.	DEBIT	CREDIT	CREDIT BALANCE
20-- May	1	Balance	✔			1 4 7 2 00

vendor Pittman Supply Co.   VENDOR NO. 260

DATE		ITEM	POST. REF.	DEBIT	CREDIT	CREDIT BALANCE
20-- May	1	Balance	✔			1 7 9 00

vendor Sanders Company   VENDOR NO. 280

DATE		ITEM	POST. REF.	DEBIT	CREDIT	CREDIT BALANCE
20-- May	1	Balance	✔			5 6 2 00

VENDOR   VENDOR NO.

DATE		ITEM	POST. REF.	DEBIT	CREDIT	CREDIT BALANCE

VENDOR   VENDOR NO.

DATE		ITEM	POST. REF.	DEBIT	CREDIT	CREDIT BALANCE

18-1 APPLICATION PROBLEM, p. 477

Journalizing and posting purchase on account transactions

1., 2., 3.

PURCHASES JOURNAL   PAGE 6

	DATE		ACCOUNT CREDITED	PURCH. NO.	POST. REF.	PURCHASES DR. ACCTS. PAY. CR.	
1							1
2							2
3							3
4							4
5							5
6							6
7							7
8							8
9							9
10							10
11							11
12							12
13							13
14							14
15							15
16							16
17							17
18							18
19							19
20							20
21							21
22							22
23							23
24							24
25							25
26							26
27							27
28							28
29							29
30							30
31							31
32							32

Extra form

PURCHASES JOURNAL

	DATE		ACCOUNT CREDITED	PURCH. NO.	POST. REF.	PURCHASES DR. ACCTS. PAY. CR.	
1							1
2							2
3							3
4							4
5							5
6							6
7							7
8							8
9							9
10							10
11							11
12							12
13							13
14							14
15							15
16							16
17							17
18							18
19							19
20							20
21							21
22							22
23							23
24							24
25							25
26							26
27							27
28							28
29							29
30							30
31							31
32							32
33							33

18-1 APPLICATION PROBLEM (concluded)

3. GENERAL LEDGER

ACCOUNT Accounts Payable   ACCOUNT NO. 2115

DATE		ITEM	POST. REF.	DEBIT	CREDIT	BALANCE DEBIT	BALANCE CREDIT
20-- June	1	Balance	✔				12 672 00

ACCOUNT Purchases   ACCOUNT NO. 5105

DATE		ITEM	POST. REF.	DEBIT	CREDIT	BALANCE DEBIT	BALANCE CREDIT
20-- June	1	Balance	✔			47 971 00	

2. ACCOUNTS PAYABLE LEDGER

VENDOR Daniels Company   VENDOR NO. 210

DATE		ITEM	POST. REF.	DEBIT	CREDIT	CREDIT BALANCE
20-- June	1	Balance	✔			1 69 00

VENDOR Perkins Supply   VENDOR NO. 260

DATE		ITEM	POST. REF.	DEBIT	CREDIT	CREDIT BALANCE
20-- June	1	Balance	✔			7 21 00

VENDOR Tompson Mfg. Co.   VENDOR NO. 290

DATE		ITEM	POST. REF.	DEBIT	CREDIT	CREDIT BALANCE
20-- June	1	Balance	✔			4 72 00

GENERAL LEDGER

ACCOUNT _____   ACCOUNT NO. _____

DATE	ITEM	POST. REF.	DEBIT	CREDIT	BALANCE	
					DEBIT	CREDIT

ACCOUNT _____   ACCOUNT NO. _____

DATE	ITEM	POST. REF.	DEBIT	CREDIT	BALANCE	
					DEBIT	CREDIT

ACCOUNTS PAYABLE LEDGER

VENDOR _____   VENDOR NO. _____

DATE	ITEM	POST. REF.	DEBIT	CREDIT	CREDIT BALANCE

VENDOR _____   VENDOR NO. _____

DATE	ITEM	POST. REF.	DEBIT	CREDIT	CREDIT BALANCE

VENDOR _____   VENDOR NO. _____

DATE	ITEM	POST. REF.	DEBIT	CREDIT	CREDIT BALANCE

18-2 APPLICATION PROBLEM, p. 477

Recording cash payments for expenses and purchases using a cash payments journal

CASH PAYMENTS JOURNAL

PAGE 21

			GENERAL		ACCOUNTS PAYABLE DEBIT	PURCHASES DISCOUNT CREDIT	CASH CREDIT
DATE	ACCOUNT TITLE	CK. NO.	POST. REF.	DEBIT	CREDIT			

Extra form

CASH PAYMENTS JOURNAL

				GENERAL		ACCOUNTS PAYABLE DEBIT	PURCHASES DISCOUNT CREDIT	CASH CREDIT
				DEBIT	CREDIT			
DATE	ACCOUNT TITLE	CK. NO.	POST. REF.	1	2	3	4	5

PAGE

18-3 APPLICATION PROBLEM, p. 478

Preparing a petty cash report

1., 2.

_____

_____

_____

_____

_____

_____

_____

_____

_____

_____

3.

PETTY CASH REPORT		
Date: _____	Custodian: _____	
Explanation	Reconciliation	Replenish Amount
Fund total		
Payments:		
_____		
_____		
_____		
Less: Total payments	_____ →	
Equals: Recorded amount on hand	_____	
Less: Actual amount on hand	_____	
Equals: Cash short (over)	_____ →	
Amount to replenish		_____

Extra forms

PETTY CASH REPORT

Date: _____   Custodian: _____

	Explanation	Reconciliation	Replenish Amount
Fund total Payments:			
Less: Total payments			
Equals: Recorded amount on hand			
Less: Actual amount on hand			
Equals: Cash short (over)			
Amount to replenish			

PETTY CASH REPORT

Date: _____   Custodian: _____

	Explanation	Reconciliation	Replenish Amount
Fund total Payments:			
Less: Total payments			
Equals: Recorded amount on hand			
Less: Actual amount on hand			
Equals: Cash short (over)			
Amount to replenish			

18-4 **APPLICATION PROBLEM, p. 478**

Journalizing and posting cash payment transactions using a cash payments journal

1., 2., 3., 4.

CASH PAYMENTS JOURNAL

PAGE 7

					GENERAL		ACCOUNTS PAYABLE DEBIT	PURCHASES DISCOUNT CREDIT	CASH CREDIT
DATE	ACCOUNT TITLE	CK. NO.	POST. REF.		DEBIT	CREDIT			
1				1		2	3	4	5

Extra form

CASH PAYMENTS JOURNAL

DATE	ACCOUNT TITLE	CK. NO.	POST. REF.	GENERAL DEBIT	GENERAL CREDIT	ACCOUNTS PAYABLE DEBIT	PURCHASES DISCOUNT CREDIT	CASH CREDIT
				1	2	3	4	5

18-4 APPLICATION PROBLEM (continued)

3., 4.   **GENERAL LEDGER**

ACCOUNT Cash   ACCOUNT NO. 1105

DATE		ITEM	POST. REF.	DEBIT	CREDIT	BALANCE	
						DEBIT	CREDIT
July 1		Balance	✔			12 7 1 6 90	

ACCOUNT Petty Cash   ACCOUNT NO. 1110

DATE		ITEM	POST. REF.	DEBIT	CREDIT	BALANCE	
						DEBIT	CREDIT
July 1		Balance	✔			2 0 0 00	

ACCOUNT Supplies   ACCOUNT NO. 1140

DATE		ITEM	POST. REF.	DEBIT	CREDIT	BALANCE	
						DEBIT	CREDIT
July 1		Balance	✔			2 6 4 7 00	

ACCOUNT Accounts Payable   ACCOUNT NO. 2115

DATE		ITEM	POST. REF.	DEBIT	CREDIT	BALANCE	
						DEBIT	CREDIT
July 1		Balance	✔				12 9 7 3 50

ACCOUNT Purchases   ACCOUNT NO. 5105

DATE		ITEM	POST. REF.	DEBIT	CREDIT	BALANCE	
						DEBIT	CREDIT
July 1		Balance	✔			54 7 9 1 60	

ACCOUNT Purchases Discount   ACCOUNT NO. 5110

DATE		ITEM	POST. REF.	DEBIT	CREDIT	BALANCE	
						DEBIT	CREDIT
July 1		Balance	✔				6 7 1 60

3., 4.   **GENERAL LEDGER**

ACCOUNT Advertising Expense   ACCOUNT NO. 6105

DATE		ITEM	POST. REF.	DEBIT	CREDIT	BALANCE	
						DEBIT	CREDIT
July 1	Balance		✔			2 7 6 8 00	

ACCOUNT Cash Short and Over   ACCOUNT NO. 6115

DATE		ITEM	POST. REF.	DEBIT	CREDIT	BALANCE	
						DEBIT	CREDIT
July 1	Balance		✔			7 60	

ACCOUNT Miscellaneous Expense   ACCOUNT NO. 6135

DATE		ITEM	POST. REF.	DEBIT	CREDIT	BALANCE	
						DEBIT	CREDIT
July 1	Balance		✔			9 7 4 10	

ACCOUNT Rent Expense   ACCOUNT NO. 6145

DATE		ITEM	POST. REF.	DEBIT	CREDIT	BALANCE	
						DEBIT	CREDIT
July 1	Balance		✔			3 6 0 0 00	

2.   **ACCOUNTS PAYABLE LEDGER**

VENDOR Argo Company   VENDOR NO. 210

DATE		ITEM	POST. REF.	DEBIT	CREDIT	CREDIT BALANCE
July 1	Balance		✔			3 5 0 3 00

VENDOR Catwell Company   VENDOR NO. 220

DATE		ITEM	POST. REF.	DEBIT	CREDIT	CREDIT BALANCE
July 1	Balance		✔			1 3 6 4 60

18-5 APPLICATION PROBLEM, p. 479

Journalizing and posting transactions using a general journal

1., 2.

GENERAL JOURNAL

	DATE	ACCOUNT TITLE	DOC. NO.	POST. REF.	DEBIT	CREDIT	
1							1
2							2
3							3
4							4
5							5
6							6
7							7
8							8
9							9
10							10
11							11
12							12
13							13
14							14
15							15
16							16
17							17
18							18
19							19
20							20
21							21
22							22
23							23
24							24
25							25
26							26
27							27
28							28
29							29
30							30
31							31
32							32

3.

18-5 APPLICATION PROBLEM (continued)

2. GENERAL LEDGER

ACCOUNT Supplies   ACCOUNT NO. 1140

DATE	ITEM	POST. REF.	DEBIT	CREDIT	BALANCE DEBIT	BALANCE CREDIT
20-- Aug. 1	Balance	✔			2 7 9 0 00	

ACCOUNT Office Equipment   ACCOUNT NO. 1205

DATE	ITEM	POST. REF.	DEBIT	CREDIT	BALANCE DEBIT	BALANCE CREDIT
20-- Aug. 1	Balance	✔			12 7 6 9 00	

ACCOUNT Store Equipment   ACCOUNT NO. 1215

DATE	ITEM	POST. REF.	DEBIT	CREDIT	BALANCE DEBIT	BALANCE CREDIT
20-- Aug. 1	Balance	✔			18 7 0 9 00	

ACCOUNT Accounts Payable   ACCOUNT NO. 2115

DATE	ITEM	POST. REF.	DEBIT	CREDIT	BALANCE DEBIT	BALANCE CREDIT
20-- Aug. 1	Balance	✔				5 0 2 7 00

ACCOUNT Purchases Returns and Allowances   ACCOUNT NO. 5115

DATE	ITEM	POST. REF.	DEBIT	CREDIT	BALANCE DEBIT	BALANCE CREDIT
20-- Aug. 1	Balance	✔				6 7 8 00

2., 3.   **ACCOUNTS PAYABLE LEDGER**

VENDOR Cantrell Company   VENDOR NO. 210

DATE	ITEM	POST. REF.	DEBIT	CREDIT	CREDIT BALANCE
20-- Aug. 1	Balance	✓			2 6 4 7 00

VENDOR David Manufacturing   VENDOR NO. 220

DATE	ITEM	POST. REF.	DEBIT	CREDIT	CREDIT BALANCE
20-- Aug. 1	Balance	✓			8 0 9 00

VENDOR Flick, Inc.   VENDOR NO. 230

DATE	ITEM	POST. REF.	DEBIT	CREDIT	CREDIT BALANCE
20-- Aug. 1	Balance	✓			6 9 7 00

VENDOR Office Solutions   VENDOR NO. 240

DATE	ITEM	POST. REF.	DEBIT	CREDIT	CREDIT BALANCE
20-- Aug. 1	Balance	✓			8 7 4 00

VENDOR   VENDOR NO.

DATE	ITEM	POST. REF.	DEBIT	CREDIT	CREDIT BALANCE

18-6 APPLICATION PROBLEM, p. 479

Journalizing and posting purchases transactions

1., 2.

PURCHASES JOURNAL   PAGE 9

	DATE	ACCOUNT CREDITED	PURCH. NO.	POST. REF.	PURCHASES DR. ACCTS. PAY. CR.	
1						1
2						2
3						3
4						4
5						5
6						6
7						7
8						8
9						9
10						10
11						11
12						12

1., 2.

GENERAL JOURNAL   PAGE 9

	DATE	ACCOUNT TITLE	DOC. NO.	POST. REF.	DEBIT	CREDIT	
1							1
2							2
3							3
4							4
5							5
6							6
7							7
8							8
9							9
10							10
11							11
12							12

1., 2.

CASH PAYMENTS JOURNAL

PAGE 17

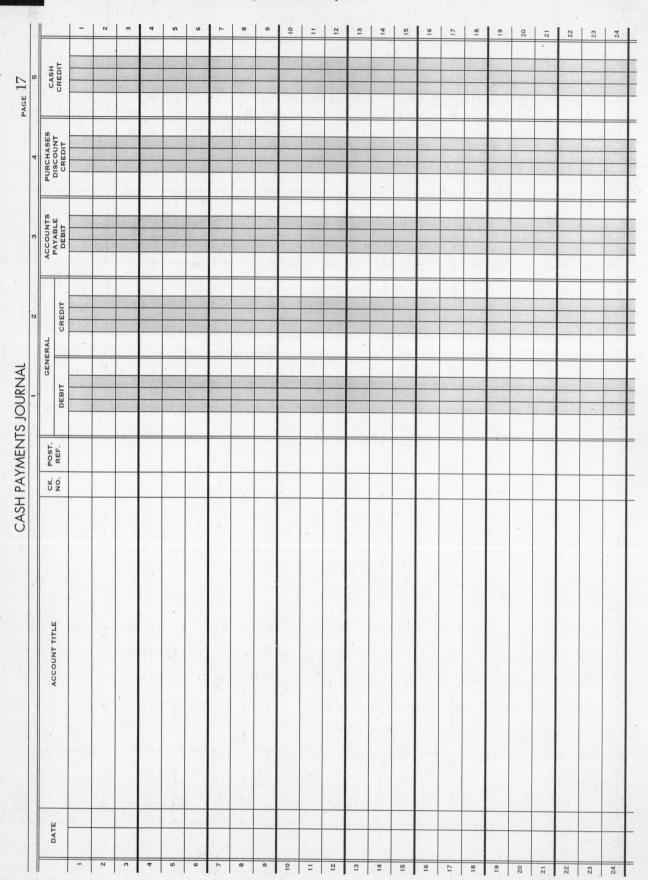

18-6 APPLICATION PROBLEM (continued)

2.   **GENERAL LEDGER**

ACCOUNT Cash   ACCOUNT NO. 1105

DATE		ITEM	POST. REF.	DEBIT	CREDIT	BALANCE	
						DEBIT	CREDIT
Sept. 20--	1	Balance	✔			12 7 2 6 00	

ACCOUNT Accounts Payable   ACCOUNT NO. 2115

DATE		ITEM	POST. REF.	DEBIT	CREDIT	BALANCE	
						DEBIT	CREDIT
Sept. 20--	1	Balance	✔				7 1 1 9 00

ACCOUNT Purchases   ACCOUNT NO. 5105

DATE		ITEM	POST. REF.	DEBIT	CREDIT	BALANCE	
						DEBIT	CREDIT
Sept. 20--	1	Balance	✔			51 9 1 3 00	

ACCOUNT Purchases Discount   ACCOUNT NO. 5110

DATE		ITEM	POST. REF.	DEBIT	CREDIT	BALANCE	
						DEBIT	CREDIT
Sept. 20--	1	Balance	✔				4 7 9 10

ACCOUNT Purchases Returns and Allowances   ACCOUNT NO. 5115

DATE		ITEM	POST. REF.	DEBIT	CREDIT	BALANCE	
						DEBIT	CREDIT
Sept. 20--	1	Balance	✔				3 8 7 1 00

2.

ACCOUNTS PAYABLE LEDGER

VENDOR Bell Supply   VENDOR NO. 240

DATE	ITEM	POST. REF.	DEBIT	CREDIT	CREDIT BALANCE

VENDOR Brandon Company   VENDOR NO. 250

DATE	ITEM	POST. REF.	DEBIT	CREDIT	CREDIT BALANCE

VENDOR   VENDOR NO.

DATE	ITEM	POST. REF.	DEBIT	CREDIT	CREDIT BALANCE

VENDOR   VENDOR NO.

DATE	ITEM	POST. REF.	DEBIT	CREDIT	CREDIT BALANCE

VENDOR   VENDOR NO.

DATE	ITEM	POST. REF.	DEBIT	CREDIT	CREDIT BALANCE

18-7 MASTERY PROBLEM, p. 480

Journalizing and posting purchases and cash payment transactions

1., 2.

PURCHASES JOURNAL   PAGE 11

	DATE		ACCOUNT CREDITED	PURCH. NO.	POST. REF.	PURCHASES DR. ACCTS. PAY. CR.	
1							1
2							2
3							3
4							4
5							5
6							6
7							7
8							8
9							9
10							10
11							11
12							12

1.

GENERAL JOURNAL   PAGE 11

	DATE		ACCOUNT TITLE	DOC. NO.	POST. REF.	DEBIT	CREDIT	
1								1
2								2
3								3
4								4
5								5
6								6
7								7
8								8
9								9
10								10
11								11
12								12

1., 3.

CASH PAYMENTS JOURNAL

PAGE 21

DATE	ACCOUNT TITLE	CK. NO.	POST. REF.	GENERAL DEBIT	GENERAL CREDIT	ACCOUNTS PAYABLE DEBIT	PURCHASES DISCOUNT CREDIT	CASH CREDIT

18-7 MASTERY PROBLEM (continued)

4.

1., 2., 3., 4.   **GENERAL LEDGER**

ACCOUNT Cash   ACCOUNT NO. 1105

DATE	ITEM	POST. REF.	DEBIT	CREDIT	BALANCE DEBIT	BALANCE CREDIT
Nov. 1	Balance	✔			12 7 1 7 00	

ACCOUNT Petty Cash   ACCOUNT NO. 1110

DATE	ITEM	POST. REF.	DEBIT	CREDIT	BALANCE DEBIT	BALANCE CREDIT
Nov. 1	Balance	✔			2 0 0 00	

ACCOUNT Supplies   ACCOUNT NO. 1140

DATE	ITEM	POST. REF.	DEBIT	CREDIT	BALANCE DEBIT	BALANCE CREDIT
Nov. 1	Balance	✔			3 1 0 6 00	

ACCOUNT Accounts Payable   ACCOUNT NO. 2115

DATE	ITEM	POST. REF.	DEBIT	CREDIT	BALANCE DEBIT	BALANCE CREDIT
Nov. 1	Balance	✔				3 7 7 2 00

ACCOUNT Purchases   ACCOUNT NO. 5105

DATE	ITEM	POST. REF.	DEBIT	CREDIT	BALANCE DEBIT	BALANCE CREDIT
Nov. 1	Balance	✔			62 7 3 4 10	

18-7 MASTERY PROBLEM (continued)

1., 2., 3., 4. GENERAL LEDGER

ACCOUNT Purchases Discount ACCOUNT NO. 5110

DATE	ITEM	POST. REF.	DEBIT	CREDIT	BALANCE DEBIT	BALANCE CREDIT
20-- Nov. 1	Balance	✔				1 0 9 2 70

ACCOUNT Purchases Returns and Allowances ACCOUNT NO. 5115

DATE	ITEM	POST. REF.	DEBIT	CREDIT	BALANCE DEBIT	BALANCE CREDIT
20-- Nov. 1	Balance	✔				4 9 7 5 50

ACCOUNT Advertising Expense ACCOUNT NO. 6105

DATE	ITEM	POST. REF.	DEBIT	CREDIT	BALANCE DEBIT	BALANCE CREDIT
20-- Nov. 1	Balance	✔			3 7 9 2 00	

ACCOUNT Cash Short and Over ACCOUNT NO. 6110

DATE	ITEM	POST. REF.	DEBIT	CREDIT	BALANCE DEBIT	BALANCE CREDIT
20-- Nov. 1	Balance	✔			3 13	

ACCOUNT Miscellaneous Expense ACCOUNT NO. 6135

DATE	ITEM	POST. REF.	DEBIT	CREDIT	BALANCE DEBIT	BALANCE CREDIT
20-- Nov. 1	Balance	✔			2 1 9 2 16	

ACCOUNT Rent Expense ACCOUNT NO. 6145

DATE	ITEM	POST. REF.	DEBIT	CREDIT	BALANCE DEBIT	BALANCE CREDIT
20-- Nov. 1	Balance	✔			5 0 0 0 00	

1., 4. **ACCOUNTS PAYABLE LEDGER**

VENDOR Bennett Supply   VENDOR NO. 210

DATE	ITEM	POST. REF.	DEBIT	CREDIT	CREDIT BALANCE
20-- Nov. 1	Balance	✔			1 2 6 9 00

VENDOR Black, Inc.   VENDOR NO. 220

DATE	ITEM	POST. REF.	DEBIT	CREDIT	CREDIT BALANCE

VENDOR Ford Supply   VENDOR NO. 230

DATE	ITEM	POST. REF.	DEBIT	CREDIT	CREDIT BALANCE

VENDOR Riddell Pipe Company   VENDOR NO. 240

DATE	ITEM	POST. REF.	DEBIT	CREDIT	CREDIT BALANCE

VENDOR Wells Company   VENDOR NO. 250

DATE	ITEM	POST. REF.	DEBIT	CREDIT	CREDIT BALANCE
20-- Nov. 1	Balance	✔			2 5 0 3 00

18-8 CHALLENGE PROBLEM, p. 481

Journalizing transactions in a combined purchases-cash payments journal

1., 2.

PURCHASES—CASH PAYMENTS JOURNAL

PAGE 21

	DATE	ACCOUNT TITLE	DOC. NO.	POST. REF.	GENERAL DEBIT	GENERAL CREDIT	PURCHASES DEBIT	ACCOUNTS PAYABLE DEBIT	ACCOUNTS PAYABLE CREDIT	PURCHASES DISCOUNT CREDIT	CASH CREDIT
1											
2											
3											
4											
5											
6											
7											
8											
9											
10											
11											
12											
13											
14											
15											
16											
17											
18											
19											
20											
21											
22											
23											

1.

GENERAL JOURNAL PAGE 11

	DATE		ACCOUNT TITLE	DOC. NO.	POST. REF.	DEBIT	CREDIT	
1								1
2								2
3								3
4								4
5								5
6								6
7								7
8								8
9								9
10								10
11								11
12								12
13								13
14								14
15								15

3.

19-1 WORK TOGETHER, p. 492

Journalizing and posting sales on account transactions

3., 4., 5., 6.

SALES JOURNAL   PAGE 4

	DATE		ACCOUNT DEBITED	SALE NO.	POST. REF.	ACCOUNTS RECEIVABLE DEBIT	SALES CREDIT	SALES TAX PAYABLE CREDIT	
						1	2	3	
1									1
2									2
3									3
4									4
5									5
6									6
7									7
8									8
9									9
10									10
11									11
12									12
13									13
14									14
15									15
16									16
17									17
18									18
19									19
20									20
21									21
22									22
23									23
24									24
25									25
26									26
27									27
28									28
29									29
30									30
31									31
32									32

Journalizing and posting sales on account transactions

7., 8., 9., 10.

SALES JOURNAL

PAGE 6

	DATE		ACCOUNT DEBITED	SALE NO.	POST. REF.	ACCOUNTS RECEIVABLE DEBIT (1)	SALES CREDIT (2)	SALES TAX PAYABLE CREDIT (3)	
1									1
2									2
3									3
4									4
5									5
6									6
7									7
8									8
9									9
10									10
11									11
12									12
13									13
14									14
15									15
16									16
17									17
18									18
19									19
20									20
21									21
22									22
23									23
24									24
25									25
26									26
27									27
28									28
29									29
30									30
31									31
32									32

19-1 WORK TOGETHER (concluded)

6.   GENERAL LEDGER

ACCOUNT Accounts Receivable   ACCOUNT NO. 1125

DATE		ITEM	POST. REF.	DEBIT	CREDIT	BALANCE DEBIT	BALANCE CREDIT
20-- Apr.	1	Balance	✔			7 4 2 6 26	

ACCOUNT Sales Tax Payable   ACCOUNT NO. 2135

DATE		ITEM	POST. REF.	DEBIT	CREDIT	BALANCE DEBIT	BALANCE CREDIT
20-- Apr.	1	Balance	✔				1 9 4 00

ACCOUNT Sales   ACCOUNT NO. 4105

DATE		ITEM	POST. REF.	DEBIT	CREDIT	BALANCE DEBIT	BALANCE CREDIT
20-- Apr.	1	Balance	✔				10 7 9 1 60

4.   ACCOUNTS RECEIVABLE LEDGER

CUSTOMER Belmont Water Association   CUSTOMER NO. 110

DATE		ITEM	POST. REF.	DEBIT	CREDIT	DEBIT BALANCE
20-- Apr.	1	Balance	✔			3 7 1 56

CUSTOMER Blanton College   CUSTOMER NO. 120

DATE		ITEM	POST. REF.	DEBIT	CREDIT	DEBIT BALANCE
20-- Apr.	1	Balance	✔			2 7 9 1 00

CUSTOMER Northland Hospital   CUSTOMER NO. 160

DATE		ITEM	POST. REF.	DEBIT	CREDIT	DEBIT BALANCE
20-- Apr.	1	Balance	✔			3 7 9 1 80

CUSTOMER Tess & Sons   CUSTOMER NO. 190

DATE		ITEM	POST. REF.	DEBIT	CREDIT	DEBIT BALANCE
20-- Apr.	1	Balance	✔			4 7 1 90

10. **GENERAL LEDGER**

ACCOUNT Accounts Receivable   ACCOUNT NO. 1125

DATE		ITEM	POST. REF.	DEBIT	CREDIT	BALANCE	
						DEBIT	CREDIT
June 20--	1	Balance	✔			3 2 2 9 00	

ACCOUNT Sales Tax Payable   ACCOUNT NO. 2135

DATE		ITEM	POST. REF.	DEBIT	CREDIT	BALANCE	
						DEBIT	CREDIT
June 20--	1	Balance	✔				3 9 7 80

ACCOUNT Sales   ACCOUNT NO. 4105

DATE		ITEM	POST. REF.	DEBIT	CREDIT	BALANCE	
						DEBIT	CREDIT
June 20--	1	Balance	✔				36 9 8 0 10

8. **ACCOUNTS RECEIVABLE LEDGER**

CUSTOMER Gulf High School   CUSTOMER NO. 110

DATE		ITEM	POST. REF.	DEBIT	CREDIT	DEBIT BALANCE
June 20--	1	Balance	✔			6 7 9 80

CUSTOMER King Services   CUSTOMER NO. 140

DATE		ITEM	POST. REF.	DEBIT	CREDIT	DEBIT BALANCE
June 20--	1	Balance	✔			3 7 9 80

CUSTOMER Lincoln Designs   CUSTOMER NO. 150

DATE		ITEM	POST. REF.	DEBIT	CREDIT	DEBIT BALANCE
June 20--	1	Balance	✔			9 7 1 80

CUSTOMER Lynch Interiors   CUSTOMER NO. 155

DATE		ITEM	POST. REF.	DEBIT	CREDIT	DEBIT BALANCE
June 20--	1	Balance	✔			1 1 9 7 60

19-2 WORK TOGETHER, p. 498

Journalizing and posting cash receipts transactions

3., 4., 5., 6.

CASH RECEIPTS JOURNAL

PAGE 5

			1	2	3	4	5	6	7	8
			GENERAL		ACCOUNTS RECEIVABLE CREDIT	SALES CREDIT	SALES TAX PAYABLE		SALES DISCOUNT DEBIT	CASH DEBIT
DATE	ACCOUNT TITLE	DOC. NO.	POST. REF.	DEBIT	CREDIT			DEBIT	CREDIT		

Journalizing and posting cash receipts transactions

7., 8., 9., 10.

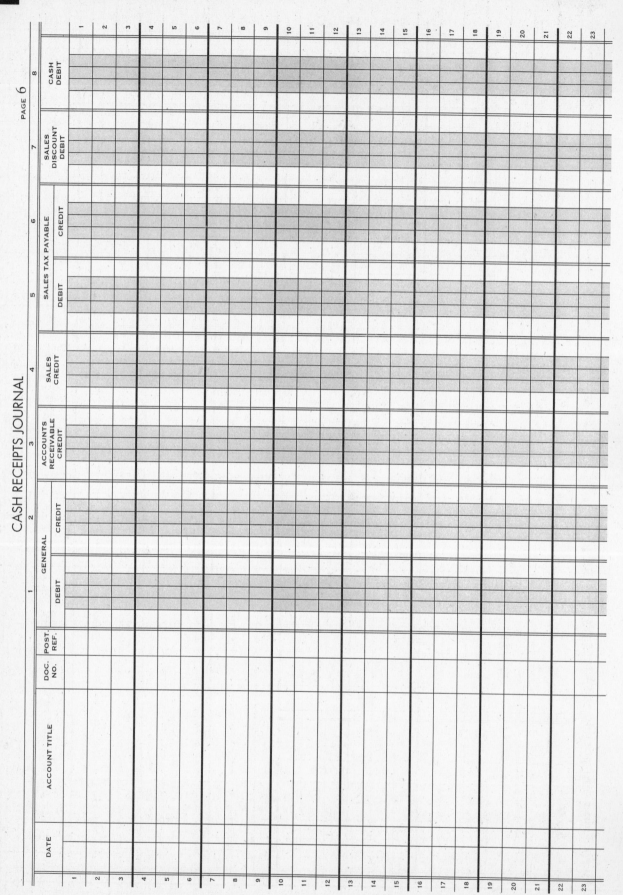

CASH RECEIPTS JOURNAL

PAGE 6

19-2 WORK TOGETHER (concluded)

6.

GENERAL LEDGER

ACCOUNT Cash   **ACCOUNT NO.** 1105

DATE		ITEM	POST. REF.	DEBIT	CREDIT	BALANCE DEBIT	BALANCE CREDIT
20-- May	1	Balance	✔			2 7 9 8 60	

ACCOUNT Accounts Receivable   **ACCOUNT NO.** 1125

DATE		ITEM	POST. REF.	DEBIT	CREDIT	BALANCE DEBIT	BALANCE CREDIT
20-- May	1	Balance	✔			4 9 7 5 00	

ACCOUNT Sales Tax Payable   **ACCOUNT NO.** 2140

DATE		ITEM	POST. REF.	DEBIT	CREDIT	BALANCE DEBIT	BALANCE CREDIT
20-- May	1	Balance	✔				1 2 6 10

ACCOUNT Sales   **ACCOUNT NO.** 4105

DATE		ITEM	POST. REF.	DEBIT	CREDIT	BALANCE DEBIT	BALANCE CREDIT
20-- May	1	Balance	✔				10 7 6 0 90

ACCOUNT Sales Discount   **ACCOUNT NO.** 4110

DATE		ITEM	POST. REF.	DEBIT	CREDIT	BALANCE DEBIT	BALANCE CREDIT
20-- May	1	Balance	✔			1 7 2 80	

4.

ACCOUNTS RECEIVABLE LEDGER

CUSTOMER Hawbecker Supply   **CUSTOMER NO.** 140

DATE		ITEM	POST. REF.	DEBIT	CREDIT	DEBIT BALANCE
20-- May	1	Balance	✔			1 5 7 00

CUSTOMER Nelson Company   **CUSTOMER NO.** 160

DATE		ITEM	POST. REF.	DEBIT	CREDIT	DEBIT BALANCE
20-- May	1	Balance	✔			3 7 9 2 00

10.

GENERAL LEDGER

ACCOUNT Cash   ACCOUNT NO. 1105

DATE		ITEM	POST. REF.	DEBIT	CREDIT	BALANCE DEBIT	BALANCE CREDIT
20-- June	1	Balance	✔			2 7 9 8 15	

ACCOUNT Accounts Receivable   ACCOUNT NO. 1125

DATE		ITEM	POST. REF.	DEBIT	CREDIT	BALANCE DEBIT	BALANCE CREDIT
20-- June	1	Balance	✔			9 9 6 50	

ACCOUNT Sales Tax Payable   ACCOUNT NO. 2140

DATE		ITEM	POST. REF.	DEBIT	CREDIT	BALANCE DEBIT	BALANCE CREDIT
20-- June	1	Balance	✔				2 0 9 60

ACCOUNT Sales   ACCOUNT NO. 4105

DATE		ITEM	POST. REF.	DEBIT	CREDIT	BALANCE DEBIT	BALANCE CREDIT
20-- June	1	Balance	✔				18 7 6 9 20

ACCOUNT Sales Discount   ACCOUNT NO. 4110

DATE		ITEM	POST. REF.	DEBIT	CREDIT	BALANCE DEBIT	BALANCE CREDIT
20-- June	1	Balance	✔			5 9 90	

8.

ACCOUNTS RECEIVABLE LEDGER

CUSTOMER Mason Insurance   CUSTOMER NO. 150

DATE		ITEM	POST. REF.	DEBIT	CREDIT	DEBIT BALANCE
20-- June	1	Balance	✔			4 9 7 00

CUSTOMER Pait Café   CUSTOMER NO. 160

DATE		ITEM	POST. REF.	DEBIT	CREDIT	DEBIT BALANCE
20-- June	1	Balance	✔			2 7 0 00

19-3 WORK TOGETHER, p. 503

Journalizing and posting transactions using a general journal

3., 4.

GENERAL JOURNAL

	DATE	ACCOUNT TITLE	DOC. NO.	POST. REF.	DEBIT	CREDIT	
1							1
2							2
3							3
4							4
5							5
6							6
7							7
8							8
9							9
10							10
11							11
12							12

5.

Journalizing and posting transactions using a general journal

6., 7.

GENERAL JOURNAL PAGE 7

	DATE	ACCOUNT TITLE	DOC. NO.	POST. REF.	DEBIT	CREDIT	
1							1
2							2
3							3
4							4
5							5
6							6
7							7
8							8
9							9
10							10
11							11
12							12

8.

19-3 WORK TOGETHER (concluded)

4.

GENERAL LEDGER

ACCOUNT Accounts Receivable   ACCOUNT NO. 1125

DATE		ITEM	POST. REF.	DEBIT	CREDIT	BALANCE DEBIT	BALANCE CREDIT
20-- June	1	Balance	✔			3 6 0 0 09	

ACCOUNT Sales Tax Payable   ACCOUNT NO. 2140

DATE		ITEM	POST. REF.	DEBIT	CREDIT	BALANCE DEBIT	BALANCE CREDIT
20-- June	1	Balance	✔				4 7 2 60

ACCOUNT Sales Returns and Allowances   ACCOUNT NO. 4115

DATE		ITEM	POST. REF.	DEBIT	CREDIT	BALANCE DEBIT	BALANCE CREDIT
20-- June	1	Balance	✔			3 9 7 6 80	

4., 5.

ACCOUNTS RECEIVABLE LEDGER

CUSTOMER D. Howell, MD   CUSTOMER NO. 140

DATE		ITEM	POST. REF.	DEBIT	CREDIT	DEBIT BALANCE

CUSTOMER Howsley Dance Studio   CUSTOMER NO. 150

DATE		ITEM	POST. REF.	DEBIT	CREDIT	DEBIT BALANCE
20-- June	1	Balance	✔			4 1 4 99

CUSTOMER Westfall High School   CUSTOMER NO. 180

DATE		ITEM	POST. REF.	DEBIT	CREDIT	DEBIT BALANCE
20-- June	1	Balance	✔			3 9 2 50

CUSTOMER Wilbanks and Associates   CUSTOMER NO. 190

DATE		ITEM	POST. REF.	DEBIT	CREDIT	DEBIT BALANCE
20-- June	1	Balance	✔			2 7 9 2 60

7.   **GENERAL LEDGER**

ACCOUNT Accounts Receivable   ACCOUNT NO. 1125

DATE		ITEM	POST. REF.	DEBIT	CREDIT	BALANCE DEBIT	BALANCE CREDIT
July	1	Balance	✔			2 6 2 1 10	

ACCOUNT Sales Tax Payable   ACCOUNT NO. 2140

DATE		ITEM	POST. REF.	DEBIT	CREDIT	BALANCE DEBIT	BALANCE CREDIT
July	1	Balance	✔				3 6 9 50

ACCOUNT Sales Returns and Allowances   ACCOUNT NO. 4115

DATE		ITEM	POST. REF.	DEBIT	CREDIT	BALANCE DEBIT	BALANCE CREDIT
July	1	Balance	✔			2 7 1 8 50	

7., 8.   **ACCOUNTS RECEIVABLE LEDGER**

CUSTOMER Brooksville High School   CUSTOMER NO. 110

DATE		ITEM	POST. REF.	DEBIT	CREDIT	DEBIT BALANCE
July	1	Balance	✔			4 7 9 80

CUSTOMER Naper Glass Co.   CUSTOMER NO. 160

DATE		ITEM	POST. REF.	DEBIT	CREDIT	DEBIT BALANCE
July	1	Balance	✔			3 7 2 60

CUSTOMER Naper Paper Co.   CUSTOMER NO. 165

DATE		ITEM	POST. REF.	DEBIT	CREDIT	DEBIT BALANCE

CUSTOMER Ulman Builders   CUSTOMER NO. 190

DATE		ITEM	POST. REF.	DEBIT	CREDIT	DEBIT BALANCE
July	1	Balance	✔			1 7 6 8 70

19-4 WORK TOGETHER, p. 509

Journalizing international sales transactions

6., 7.

CASH RECEIPTS JOURNAL

PAGE 9

			GENERAL		ACCOUNTS RECEIVABLE	SALES	SALES TAX PAYABLE		SALES DISCOUNT	CASH
DATE	ACCOUNT TITLE	DOC. NO.	POST. REF.	DEBIT	CREDIT	CREDIT	CREDIT	DEBIT	CREDIT	DEBIT	DEBIT
				1	2	3	4	5	6	7	8

GENERAL JOURNAL

PAGE 5

6.

DATE	ACCOUNT TITLE	DOC. NO.	POST. REF.	DEBIT	CREDIT
				1	

Journalizing international sales transactions

8., 9.

CASH RECEIPTS JOURNAL

PAGE 3

				1 GENERAL	2 GENERAL	3 ACCOUNTS RECEIVABLE	4 SALES	5 SALES TAX PAYABLE	6 SALES TAX PAYABLE	7 SALES DISCOUNT	8 CASH
DATE	ACCOUNT TITLE	DOC. NO.	POST. REF.	DEBIT	CREDIT	CREDIT	CREDIT	DEBIT	CREDIT	DEBIT	DEBIT
1											
2											
3											
4											
5											
6											
7											
8											
9											
10											

GENERAL JOURNAL

PAGE 2

8.

DATE	ACCOUNT TITLE	DOC. NO.	POST. REF.	DEBIT	CREDIT
1					
2					
3					
4					
5					
6					

19-1 APPLICATION PROBLEM, p. 511

Journalizing and posting sales on account transactions

1., 2., 3., 4.

SALES JOURNAL   PAGE 3

	DATE	ACCOUNT DEBITED	SALE NO.	POST. REF.	ACCOUNTS RECEIVABLE DEBIT	SALES CREDIT	SALES TAX PAYABLE CREDIT	
1								1
2								2
3								3
4								4
5								5
6								6
7								7
8								8
9								9
10								10
11								11
12								12
13								13
14								14
15								15
16								16
17								17
18								18
19								19
20								20
21								21
22								22
23								23
24								24
25								25
26								26
27								27
28								28
29								29
30								30
31								31
32								32

Extra form

SALES JOURNAL

	DATE		ACCOUNT DEBITED	SALE NO.	POST. REF.	ACCOUNTS RECEIVABLE DEBIT 1	SALES CREDIT 2	SALES TAX PAYABLE CREDIT 3	
1									1
2									2
3									3
4									4
5									5
6									6
7									7
8									8
9									9
10									10
11									11
12									12
13									13
14									14
15									15
16									16
17									17
18									18
19									19
20									20
21									21
22									22
23									23
24									24
25									25
26									26
27									27
28									28
29									29
30									30
31									31
32									32

19-1 **APPLICATION PROBLEM (continued)**

4.   **GENERAL LEDGER**

ACCOUNT Accounts Receivable   ACCOUNT NO. 1125

DATE		ITEM	POST. REF.	DEBIT	CREDIT	BALANCE	
						DEBIT	CREDIT
Mar.	1	Balance	✔			3 0 8 7 40	

ACCOUNT Sales Tax Payable   ACCOUNT NO. 2140

DATE		ITEM	POST. REF.	DEBIT	CREDIT	BALANCE	
						DEBIT	CREDIT
Mar.	1	Balance	✔				4 7 1 60

ACCOUNT Sales   ACCOUNT NO. 4105

DATE		ITEM	POST. REF.	DEBIT	CREDIT	BALANCE	
						DEBIT	CREDIT
Mar.	1	Balance	✔				12 7 9 7 50

ACCOUNT   ACCOUNT NO.

DATE		ITEM	POST. REF.	DEBIT	CREDIT	BALANCE	
						DEBIT	CREDIT

ACCOUNT   ACCOUNT NO.

DATE		ITEM	POST. REF.	DEBIT	CREDIT	BALANCE	
						DEBIT	CREDIT

2.   **ACCOUNTS RECEIVABLE LEDGER**

customer Cruz and Diaz   customer no. 110

DATE		ITEM	POST. REF.	DEBIT	CREDIT	DEBIT BALANCE
20-- Mar.	1	Balance	✔			6 9 8 70

customer Hampton University   customer no. 120

DATE		ITEM	POST. REF.	DEBIT	CREDIT	DEBIT BALANCE
20-- Mar.	1	Balance	✔			2 9 8 60

customer Maitland Supply   customer no. 130

DATE		ITEM	POST. REF.	DEBIT	CREDIT	DEBIT BALANCE
20-- Mar.	1	Balance	✔			1 9 7 60

customer Valdez and Associates   customer no. 140

DATE		ITEM	POST. REF.	DEBIT	CREDIT	DEBIT BALANCE
20-- Mar.	1	Balance	✔			1 8 9 2 50

19-2 APPLICATION PROBLEM, p. 511

Journalizing and posting cash receipts transactions

1., 2., 3., 4.

CASH RECEIPTS JOURNAL

PAGE 5

| | | | | 1 | 2 | 3 | 4 | 5 | 6 | 7 | 8 |
| | | | | GENERAL | | ACCOUNTS RECEIVABLE CREDIT | SALES CREDIT | SALES TAX PAYABLE | | SALES DISCOUNT DEBIT | CASH DEBIT |
DATE	ACCOUNT TITLE	DOC. NO.	POST. REF.	DEBIT	CREDIT			DEBIT	CREDIT		
1											
2											
3											
4											
5											
6											
7											
8											
9											
10											
11											
12											
13											
14											
15											
16											
17											
18											
19											
20											
21											
22											
23											

Extra form

CASH RECEIPTS JOURNAL

PAGE

| DATE | ACCOUNT TITLE | DOC. NO. | POST. REF. | GENERAL | | ACCOUNTS RECEIVABLE CREDIT | SALES CREDIT | SALES TAX PAYABLE | | SALES DISCOUNT DEBIT | CASH DEBIT |
				DEBIT	CREDIT			DEBIT	CREDIT		
				1	2	3	4	5	6	7	8

19-2 **APPLICATION PROBLEM (continued)**

4. **GENERAL LEDGER**

ACCOUNT Cash   ACCOUNT NO. 1105

DATE		ITEM	POST. REF.	DEBIT	CREDIT	BALANCE	
						DEBIT	CREDIT
20-- Apr.	1	Balance	✔			1 2 7 6 00	

ACCOUNT Accounts Receivable   ACCOUNT NO. 1125

DATE		ITEM	POST. REF.	DEBIT	CREDIT	BALANCE	
						DEBIT	CREDIT
20-- Apr.	1	Balance	✔			5 7 2 1 50	

ACCOUNT Sales Tax Payable   ACCOUNT NO. 2140

DATE		ITEM	POST. REF.	DEBIT	CREDIT	BALANCE	
						DEBIT	CREDIT
20-- Apr.	1	Balance	✔				3 7 2 10

ACCOUNT Sales   ACCOUNT NO. 4105

DATE		ITEM	POST. REF.	DEBIT	CREDIT	BALANCE	
						DEBIT	CREDIT
20-- Apr.	1	Balance	✔				40 7 1 7 10

ACCOUNT Sales Discount   ACCOUNT NO. 4110

DATE		ITEM	POST. REF.	DEBIT	CREDIT	BALANCE	
						DEBIT	CREDIT
20-- Apr.	1	Balance	✔			9 4 20	

2. ACCOUNTS RECEIVABLE LEDGER

CUSTOMER Fulton Supply   CUSTOMER NO. 110

DATE		ITEM	POST. REF.	DEBIT	CREDIT	DEBIT BALANCE
20-- Apr.	1	Balance	✔			972 00

CUSTOMER Lambert Company   CUSTOMER NO. 120

DATE		ITEM	POST. REF.	DEBIT	CREDIT	DEBIT BALANCE
20-- Apr.	1	Balance	✔			499 50

CUSTOMER Okora Industries   CUSTOMER NO. 130

DATE		ITEM	POST. REF.	DEBIT	CREDIT	DEBIT BALANCE
20-- Apr.	1	Balance	✔			459 00

CUSTOMER Westbrook Company   CUSTOMER NO. 140

DATE		ITEM	POST. REF.	DEBIT	CREDIT	DEBIT BALANCE
20-- Apr.	1	Balance	✔			3791 00

19-3 APPLICATION PROBLEM, p. 512

Journalizing and posting transactions using a general journal

1., 2.

GENERAL JOURNAL   PAGE 7

	DATE	ACCOUNT TITLE	DOC. NO.	POST. REF.	DEBIT	CREDIT	
1							1
2							2
3							3
4							4
5							5
6							6
7							7
8							8
9							9
10							10
11							11
12							12
13							13
14							14
15							15
16							16
17							17
18							18
19							19
20							20
21							21
22							22
23							23
24							24
25							25
26							26
27							27
28							28
29							29
30							30
31							31
32							32

3.

19-3 APPLICATION PROBLEM (continued)

2., 3.   **GENERAL LEDGER**

ACCOUNT Accounts Receivable   ACCOUNT NO. 1125

DATE	ITEM	POST. REF.	DEBIT	CREDIT	BALANCE DEBIT	BALANCE CREDIT
20-- July 1	Balance	✔			10 9 4 4 59	

ACCOUNT Sales Tax Payable   ACCOUNT NO. 2140

DATE	ITEM	POST. REF.	DEBIT	CREDIT	BALANCE DEBIT	BALANCE CREDIT
20-- July 1	Balance	✔				1 9 7 0 80

ACCOUNT Sales Returns and Allowances   ACCOUNT NO. 4115

DATE	ITEM	POST. REF.	DEBIT	CREDIT	BALANCE DEBIT	BALANCE CREDIT
20-- July 1	Balance	✔			5 2 9 4 70	

ACCOUNTS RECEIVABLE LEDGER

CUSTOMER Farris Industries   CUSTOMER NO. 110

DATE	ITEM	POST. REF.	DEBIT	CREDIT	DEBIT BALANCE
20-- July 1	Balance	✔			3 3 7 23

CUSTOMER Humber Crafts   CUSTOMER NO. 120

DATE	ITEM	POST. REF.	DEBIT	CREDIT	DEBIT BALANCE
20-- July 1	Balance	✔			2 7 6 1 90

2., 3.   **ACCOUNTS RECEIVABLE LEDGER**

CUSTOMER Norris Industries   CUSTOMER NO. 130

DATE		ITEM	POST. REF.	DEBIT	CREDIT	DEBIT BALANCE

CUSTOMER Osborne Middle School   CUSTOMER NO. 140

DATE		ITEM	POST. REF.	DEBIT	CREDIT	DEBIT BALANCE
20-- July	1	Balance	✔			9 2 8 50

CUSTOMER Pines Company   CUSTOMER NO. 150

DATE		ITEM	POST. REF.	DEBIT	CREDIT	DEBIT BALANCE
20-- July	1	Balance	✔			9 0 7 25

CUSTOMER Pineston, Inc.   CUSTOMER NO. 160

DATE		ITEM	POST. REF.	DEBIT	CREDIT	DEBIT BALANCE
20-- July	1	Balance	✔			1 5 3 36

CUSTOMER Rhone Company   CUSTOMER NO. 170

DATE		ITEM	POST. REF.	DEBIT	CREDIT	DEBIT BALANCE
20-- July	1	Balance	✔			5 2 7 6 90

CUSTOMER Summer & Moss   CUSTOMER NO. 180

DATE		ITEM	POST. REF.	DEBIT	CREDIT	DEBIT BALANCE
20-- July	1	Balance	✔			5 7 9 45

19-4 APPLICATION PROBLEM, p. 512

Journalizing international sales transactions

1., 2.

CASH RECEIPTS JOURNAL

PAGE 10

				1	2	3	4	5	6	7	8
				GENERAL		ACCOUNTS RECEIVABLE CREDIT	SALES CREDIT	SALES TAX PAYABLE		SALES DISCOUNT DEBIT	CASH DEBIT
DATE	ACCOUNT TITLE	DOC. NO.	POST. REF.	DEBIT	CREDIT			DEBIT	CREDIT		
1											
2											
3											
4											
5											
6											
7											
8											
9											
10											
11											
12											
13											
14											
15											
16											
17											
18											
19											
20											
21											
22											
23											

1.

GENERAL JOURNAL   PAGE 6

	DATE	ACCOUNT TITLE	DOC. NO.	POST. REF.	DEBIT	CREDIT	
1							1
2							2
3							3
4							4
5							5
6							6
7							7
8							8
9							9
10							10
11							11
12							12
13							13
14							14
15							15
16							16
17							17
18							18
19							19
20							20
21							21
22							22
23							23
24							24
25							25
26							26
27							27
28							28
29							29
30							30
31							31
32							32
33							33

19-5 APPLICATION PROBLEM, p. 513

Journalizing sales transactions

SALES JOURNAL   PAGE 2

	DATE	ACCOUNT DEBITED	SALE NO.	POST. REF.	ACCOUNTS RECEIVABLE DEBIT (1)	SALES CREDIT (2)	SALES TAX PAYABLE CREDIT (3)	
1								1
2								2
3								3
4								4
5								5
6								6
7								7
8								8
9								9
10								10
11								11
12								12

GENERAL JOURNAL   PAGE 2

	DATE	ACCOUNT TITLE	DOC. NO.	POST. REF.	DEBIT	CREDIT	
1							1
2							2
3							3
4							4
5							5
6							6
7							7
8							8
9							9
10							10
11							11
12							12

CASH RECEIPTS JOURNAL

PAGE 2

DATE	ACCOUNT TITLE	DOC. NO.	POST. REF.	GENERAL DEBIT	GENERAL CREDIT	ACCOUNTS RECEIVABLE CREDIT	SALES CREDIT	SALES TAX PAYABLE DEBIT	SALES TAX PAYABLE CREDIT	SALES DISCOUNT DEBIT	CASH DEBIT

19-6 MASTERY PROBLEM, p. 513

Journalizing and posting sales transactions

1., 2., 3.

SALES JOURNAL   PAGE 2

	DATE	ACCOUNT DEBITED	SALE NO.	POST. REF.	1 ACCOUNTS RECEIVABLE DEBIT	2 SALES CREDIT	3 SALES TAX PAYABLE CREDIT	
1								1
2								2
3								3
4								4
5								5
6								6
7								7

1.

GENERAL JOURNAL   PAGE 2

	DATE	ACCOUNT TITLE	DOC. NO.	POST. REF.	DEBIT	CREDIT	
1							1
2							2
3							3
4							4
5							5
6							6
7							7
8							8
9							9
10							10
11							11
12							12
13							13
14							14
15							15
16							16
17							17
18							18

1., 4., 5.

CASH RECEIPTS JOURNAL

PAGE 2

							1		2		3		4		5		6		7		8
DATE	ACCOUNT TITLE	DOC. NO.	POST. REF.		GENERAL				ACCOUNTS RECEIVABLE CREDIT		SALES CREDIT		SALES TAX PAYABLE			SALES DISCOUNT DEBIT		CASH DEBIT	
				DEBIT		CREDIT							DEBIT		CREDIT					

19-6 MASTERY PROBLEM (continued)

1., 3., 5., 6.   **GENERAL LEDGER**

ACCOUNT Cash   ACCOUNT NO. 1105

DATE	ITEM	POST. REF.	DEBIT	CREDIT	BALANCE DEBIT	BALANCE CREDIT
Feb. 1	Balance	✔			6 7 1 6 86	

ACCOUNT Accounts Receivable   ACCOUNT NO. 1125

DATE	ITEM	POST. REF.	DEBIT	CREDIT	BALANCE DEBIT	BALANCE CREDIT
Feb. 1	Balance	✔			4 1 9 7 86	

ACCOUNT Time Drafts Receivable   ACCOUNT NO. 1130

DATE	ITEM	POST. REF.	DEBIT	CREDIT	BALANCE DEBIT	BALANCE CREDIT
Feb. 1	Balance	✔			31 0 0 0 00	

ACCOUNT Sales Tax Payable   ACCOUNT NO. 2140

DATE	ITEM	POST. REF.	DEBIT	CREDIT	BALANCE DEBIT	BALANCE CREDIT
Feb. 1	Balance	✔				8 4 5 40

1., 3., 5., 6.   **GENERAL LEDGER**

ACCOUNT Sales   ACCOUNT NO. 4105

DATE		ITEM	POST. REF.	DEBIT	CREDIT	BALANCE DEBIT	BALANCE CREDIT
20-- Feb.	1	Balance	✔				25 781 80

ACCOUNT Sales Discount   ACCOUNT NO. 4110

DATE		ITEM	POST. REF.	DEBIT	CREDIT	BALANCE DEBIT	BALANCE CREDIT
20-- Feb.	1	Balance	✔			3 8 10	

ACCOUNT Sales Returns and Allowances   ACCOUNT NO. 4115

DATE		ITEM	POST. REF.	DEBIT	CREDIT	BALANCE DEBIT	BALANCE CREDIT
20-- Feb.	1	Balance	✔			1 89 70	

ACCOUNT   ACCOUNT NO.

DATE	ITEM	POST. REF.	DEBIT	CREDIT	BALANCE DEBIT	BALANCE CREDIT

ACCOUNT   ACCOUNT NO.

DATE	ITEM	POST. REF.	DEBIT	CREDIT	BALANCE DEBIT	BALANCE CREDIT

19-6 MASTERY PROBLEM (continued)

1., 6.

ACCOUNTS RECEIVABLE LEDGER

CUSTOMER Carol Box   CUSTOMER NO. 110

DATE	ITEM	POST. REF.	DEBIT	CREDIT	DEBIT BALANCE

CUSTOMER Maxwell, Inc.   CUSTOMER NO. 120

DATE	ITEM	POST. REF.	DEBIT	CREDIT	DEBIT BALANCE
Feb. 1	Balance	✔			491 70

CUSTOMER Platter Company   CUSTOMER NO. 130

DATE	ITEM	POST. REF.	DEBIT	CREDIT	DEBIT BALANCE
Feb. 1	Balance	✔			432 00

CUSTOMER Josh Prescott   CUSTOMER NO. 140

DATE	ITEM	POST. REF.	DEBIT	CREDIT	DEBIT BALANCE
Feb. 1	Balance	✔			389 60

CUSTOMER Howard Price   CUSTOMER NO. 150

DATE	ITEM	POST. REF.	DEBIT	CREDIT	DEBIT BALANCE
Feb. 1	Balance	✔			544 86

1., 6.   **ACCOUNTS RECEIVABLE LEDGER**

CUSTOMER James Purden

CUSTOMER NO. 160

DATE		ITEM	POST. REF.	DEBIT	CREDIT	DEBIT BALANCE
20-- Feb.	1	Balance	✔			2 8 3 50

CUSTOMER Raulston, Inc.

CUSTOMER NO. 170

DATE		ITEM	POST. REF.	DEBIT	CREDIT	DEBIT BALANCE
20-- Feb.	1	Balance	✔			4 6 10

CUSTOMER Read Company

CUSTOMER NO. 180

DATE		ITEM	POST. REF.	DEBIT	CREDIT	DEBIT BALANCE

CUSTOMER Reed, Inc.

CUSTOMER NO. 190

DATE		ITEM	POST. REF.	DEBIT	CREDIT	DEBIT BALANCE
20-- Feb.	1	Balance	✔			2 4 1 00

CUSTOMER Washington High School

CUSTOMER NO. 195

DATE		ITEM	POST. REF.	DEBIT	CREDIT	DEBIT BALANCE
20-- Feb.	1	Balance	✔			1 7 6 9 10

19-6 MASTERY PROBLEM (concluded)

6.

19-7 CHALLENGE PROBLEM, p. 515

Journalizing and posting sales, purchases, cash receipts, and cash payments transactions

1., 2.

SALES JOURNAL   PAGE 4

	DATE	ACCOUNT DEBITED	SALE NO.	POST. REF.	1 ACCOUNTS RECEIVABLE DEBIT	2 SALES CREDIT	3 SALES TAX PAYABLE CREDIT	
1								1
2								2
3								3
4								4
5								5
6								6
7								7
8								8
9								9
10								10
11								11
12								12
13								13
14								14
15								15
16								16
17								17
18								18
19								19
20								20
21								21
22								22
23								23
24								24
25								25
26								26
27								27
28								28
29								29
30								30
31								31

1., 3.

PURCHASES JOURNAL

	DATE	ACCOUNT·CREDITED	PURCH. NO.	POST. REF.	PURCHASES DR. ACCTS. PAY. CR.	
1						1
2						2
3						3
4						4
5						5
6						6
7						7
8						8
9						9
10						10
11						11
12						12
13						13

1.

GENERAL JOURNAL

	DATE	ACCOUNT TITLE	DOC. NO.	POST. REF.	DEBIT	CREDIT	
1							1
2							2
3							3
4							4
5							5
6							6
7							7
8							8
9							9
10							10
11							11
12							12
13							13

19-7 CHALLENGE PROBLEM (continued)

1., 4.

CASH RECEIPTS JOURNAL

PAGE 4

					1	2	3	4	5	6	7	8
DATE	ACCOUNT TITLE	DOC. NO.	POST. REF.		GENERAL DEBIT	GENERAL CREDIT	ACCOUNTS RECEIVABLE CREDIT	SALES CREDIT	SALES TAX PAYABLE DEBIT	SALES TAX PAYABLE CREDIT	SALES DISCOUNT DEBIT	CASH DEBIT
				1								
				2								
				3								
				4								
				5								
				6								
				7								
				8								
				9								
				10								
				11								
				12								
				13								
				14								
				15								
				16								
				17								
				18								
				19								
				20								
				21								
				22								
				23								

1., 5.

CASH PAYMENTS JOURNAL

PAGE 4

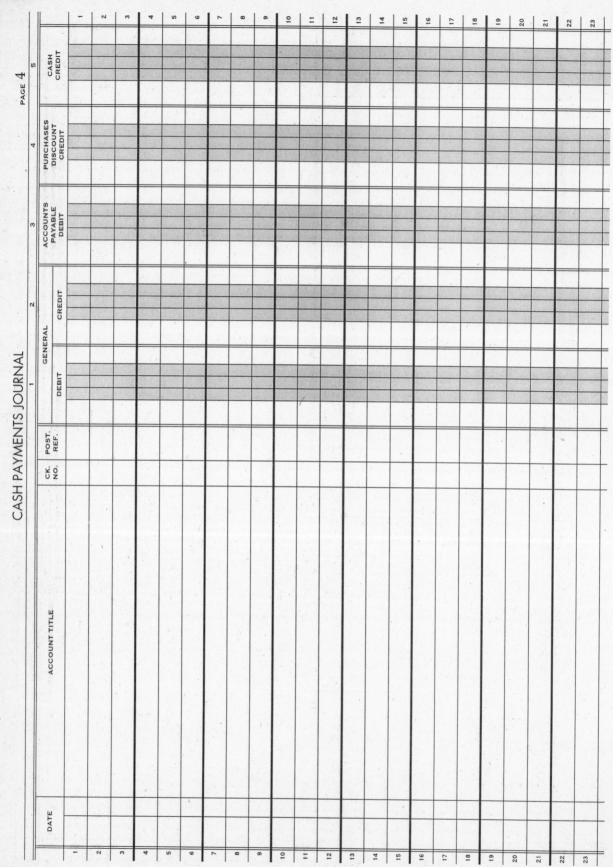

19-7 CHALLENGE PROBLEM (continued)

1., 2., 3., 4., 5., 6.   **GENERAL LEDGER**

ACCOUNT **Cash**   ACCOUNT NO. 1105

DATE		ITEM	POST. REF.	DEBIT	CREDIT	BALANCE DEBIT	BALANCE CREDIT
20-- Apr.	1	Balance	✔			3 9 2 1 80	

ACCOUNT **Petty Cash**   ACCOUNT NO. 1110

DATE		ITEM	POST. REF.	DEBIT	CREDIT	BALANCE DEBIT	BALANCE CREDIT
20-- Apr.	1	Balance	✔			3 0 0 00	

ACCOUNT **Accounts Receivable**   ACCOUNT NO. 1125

DATE		ITEM	POST. REF.	DEBIT	CREDIT	BALANCE DEBIT	BALANCE CREDIT
20-- Apr.	1	Balance	✔			1 9 6 7 48	

ACCOUNT **Supplies**   ACCOUNT NO. 1140

DATE		ITEM	POST. REF.	DEBIT	CREDIT	BALANCE DEBIT	BALANCE CREDIT
20-- Apr.	1	Balance	✔			2 4 0 00	

ACCOUNT **Accounts Payable**   ACCOUNT NO. 2115

DATE		ITEM	POST. REF.	DEBIT	CREDIT	BALANCE DEBIT	BALANCE CREDIT
20-- Apr.	1	Balance	✔				6 7 3 4 00

1., 2., 3., 4., 5., 6.   **GENERAL LEDGER**

ACCOUNT Sales Tax Payable   ACCOUNT NO. 2140

DATE	ITEM	POST. REF.	DEBIT	CREDIT	BALANCE DEBIT	BALANCE CREDIT

ACCOUNT Sales   ACCOUNT NO. 4105

DATE	ITEM	POST. REF.	DEBIT	CREDIT	BALANCE DEBIT	BALANCE CREDIT

ACCOUNT Sales Discount   ACCOUNT NO. 4110

DATE	ITEM	POST. REF.	DEBIT	CREDIT	BALANCE DEBIT	BALANCE CREDIT

ACCOUNT Sales Returns and Allowances   ACCOUNT NO. 4115

DATE	ITEM	POST. REF.	DEBIT	CREDIT	BALANCE DEBIT	BALANCE CREDIT

ACCOUNT Purchases   ACCOUNT NO. 5105

DATE	ITEM	POST. REF.	DEBIT	CREDIT	BALANCE DEBIT	BALANCE CREDIT

ACCOUNT Purchases Discount   ACCOUNT NO. 5110

DATE	ITEM	POST. REF.	DEBIT	CREDIT	BALANCE DEBIT	BALANCE CREDIT

19-7 CHALLENGE PROBLEM (continued)

1., 2., 3., 4., 5., 6.   **GENERAL LEDGER**

ACCOUNT Purchases Returns and Allowances   ACCOUNT NO. 5115

DATE	ITEM	POST. REF.	DEBIT	CREDIT	BALANCE DEBIT	BALANCE CREDIT

ACCOUNT Advertising Expense   ACCOUNT NO. 6105

DATE	ITEM	POST. REF.	DEBIT	CREDIT	BALANCE DEBIT	BALANCE CREDIT

ACCOUNT Cash Short and Over   ACCOUNT NO. 6110

DATE	ITEM	POST. REF.	DEBIT	CREDIT	BALANCE DEBIT	BALANCE CREDIT

ACCOUNT Miscellaneous Expense   ACCOUNT NO. 6130

DATE	ITEM	POST. REF.	DEBIT	CREDIT	BALANCE DEBIT	BALANCE CREDIT

ACCOUNT Rent Expense   ACCOUNT NO. 6140

DATE	ITEM	POST. REF.	DEBIT	CREDIT	BALANCE DEBIT	BALANCE CREDIT

ACCOUNT   ACCOUNT NO.

DATE	ITEM	POST. REF.	DEBIT	CREDIT	BALANCE DEBIT	BALANCE CREDIT

1., 6.   **ACCOUNTS RECEIVABLE LEDGER**

CUSTOMER Altman & Baird   CUSTOMER NO. 110

DATE		ITEM	POST. REF.	DEBIT	CREDIT	DEBIT BALANCE
20-- Apr.	1	Balance	✔			3 3 0 48

CUSTOMER Bird Company   CUSTOMER NO. 120

DATE		ITEM	POST. REF.	DEBIT	CREDIT	DEBIT BALANCE

CUSTOMER Hawbecker Company   CUSTOMER NO. 130

DATE		ITEM	POST. REF.	DEBIT	CREDIT	DEBIT BALANCE
20-- Apr.	1	Balance	✔			6 9 7 40

CUSTOMER Jenkins Co.   CUSTOMER NO. 140

DATE		ITEM	POST. REF.	DEBIT	CREDIT	DEBIT BALANCE
20-- Apr.	1	Balance	✔			6 4 8 00

CUSTOMER Parker Supply   CUSTOMER NO. 150

DATE		ITEM	POST. REF.	DEBIT	CREDIT	DEBIT BALANCE
20-- Apr.	1	Balance	✔			2 9 1 60

19-7 CHALLENGE PROBLEM (continued)

1., 6.   **ACCOUNTS PAYABLE LEDGER**

VENDOR Drake Supplies   VENDOR NO. 210

DATE	ITEM	POST. REF.	DEBIT	CREDIT	CREDIT BALANCE
20-- Apr. 1	Balance	✔			1 4 1 3 00

VENDOR Grath Electric Co.   VENDOR NO. 220

DATE	ITEM	POST. REF.	DEBIT	CREDIT	CREDIT BALANCE
20-- Apr. 1	Balance	✔			1 9 4 5 00

VENDOR Randle Company   VENDOR NO. 230

DATE	ITEM	POST. REF.	DEBIT	CREDIT	CREDIT BALANCE
20-- Apr. 1	Balance	✔			3 6 6 00

VENDOR Walters, Inc.   VENDOR NO. 240

DATE	ITEM	POST. REF.	DEBIT	CREDIT	CREDIT BALANCE
20-- Apr. 1	Balance	✔			3 0 1 0 00

Extra forms

CUSTOMER _____ CUSTOMER NO. _____

	DATE	ITEM	POST. REF.	DEBIT	CREDIT	DEBIT BALANCE

CUSTOMER _____ CUSTOMER NO. _____

	DATE	ITEM	POST. REF.	DEBIT	CREDIT	DEBIT BALANCE

VENDOR _____ VENDOR NO. _____

	DATE	ITEM	POST. REF.	DEBIT	CREDIT	CREDIT BALANCE

VENDOR _____ VENDOR NO. _____

	DATE	ITEM	POST. REF.	DEBIT	CREDIT	CREDIT BALANCE

19-7 **CHALLENGE PROBLEM (concluded)**

6.

6.

REINFORCEMENT ACTIVITY 3 PART A, p. 520

An Accounting Cycle for a Corporation: Journalizing and Posting Transactions

1., 4., 5.

SALES JOURNAL   PAGE 12

	DATE	ACCOUNT DEBITED	SALE NO.	POST. REF.	1 ACCOUNTS RECEIVABLE DEBIT	2 SALES CREDIT	3 SALES TAX PAYABLE CREDIT	
1								1
2								2
3								3
4								4
5								5
6								6
7								7
8								8
9								9
10								10
11								11
12								12

1., 4., 6.

PURCHASES JOURNAL   PAGE 12

	DATE	ACCOUNT CREDITED	PURCH. NO.	POST. REF.	PURCHASES DR. ACCTS. PAY. CR.	
1						1
2						2
3						3
4						4
5						5
6						6
7						7
8						8
9						9
10						10
11						11
12						12

1., 4.

GENERAL JOURNAL   PAGE 12

	DATE	ACCOUNT TITLE	DOC. NO.	POST. REF.	DEBIT	CREDIT	
1							1
2							2
3							3
4							4
5							5
6							6
7							7
8							8
9							9
10							10
11							11
12							12
13							13
14							14
15							15
16							16
17							17
18							18
19							19
20							20
21							21
22							22
23							23
24							24
25							25
26							26
27							27
28							28
29							29
30							30
31							31
32							32
33							33

REINFORCEMENT ACTIVITY 3 PART A (continued)

1., 4., 7., 9.

CASH RECEIPTS JOURNAL

PAGE 12

				GENERAL		ACCOUNTS RECEIVABLE CREDIT	SALES CREDIT	SALES TAX PAYABLE		SALES DISCOUNT DEBIT	CASH DEBIT
DATE	ACCOUNT TITLE	DOC. NO.	POST. REF.	DEBIT	CREDIT			DEBIT	CREDIT		
				1	2	3	4	5	6	7	8

1., 2., 3.

CASH PAYMENTS JOURNAL

PAGE 23

	DATE	ACCOUNT TITLE	CK. NO.	POST. REF.	GENERAL DEBIT	GENERAL CREDIT	ACCOUNTS PAYABLE DEBIT	PURCHASES DISCOUNT CREDIT	CASH CREDIT	
1										1
2										2
3										3
4										4
5										5
6										6
7										7
8										8
9										9
10										10
11										11
12										12
13										13
14										14
15										15
16										16
17										17
18										18
19										19
20										20
21										21
22										22
23										23
24										24
25										25

REINFORCEMENT ACTIVITY 3 PART A (continued)

1., 3., 4., 7., 10.

CASH PAYMENTS JOURNAL

PAGE 24

				1 GENERAL DEBIT	2 GENERAL CREDIT	3 ACCOUNTS PAYABLE DEBIT	4 PURCHASES DISCOUNT CREDIT	5 CASH CREDIT
DATE	ACCOUNT TITLE	CK. NO.	POST. REF.					

Extra form

CASH PAYMENTS JOURNAL

			DATE	ACCOUNT TITLE	CK. NO.	POST. REF.	GENERAL DEBIT (1)	GENERAL CREDIT (2)	ACCOUNTS PAYABLE DEBIT (3)	PURCHASES DISCOUNT CREDIT (4)	CASH CREDIT (5)	
1												1
2												2
3												3
4												4
5												5
6												6
7												7
8												8
9												9
10												10
11												11
12												12
13												13
14												14
15												15
16												16
17												17
18												18
19												19
20												20
21												21
22												22
23												23
24												24
25												25

Name _____ Date _____ Class _____

REINFORCEMENT ACTIVITY 3 PART A (continued)

The general ledger used in Reinforcement Activity 3, Part A, is needed to complete Part B.

1., 4., 5., 6., 9., 10., 11., 18., 19., 21.

GENERAL LEDGER

ACCOUNT Cash   ACCOUNT NO. 1105

DATE	ITEM	POST. REF.	DEBIT	CREDIT	BALANCE DEBIT	BALANCE CREDIT
20-- Dec. 1	Balance	✔			5 0 7 8 33	

ACCOUNT Petty Cash   ACCOUNT NO. 1110

DATE	ITEM	POST. REF.	DEBIT	CREDIT	BALANCE DEBIT	BALANCE CREDIT
20-- Dec. 1	Balance	✔			2 0 0 00	

ACCOUNT Notes Receivable   ACCOUNT NO. 1115

DATE	ITEM	POST. REF.	DEBIT	CREDIT	BALANCE DEBIT	BALANCE CREDIT
20-- Dec. 1	Balance	✔			2 8 0 0 00	

ACCOUNT Interest Receivable   ACCOUNT NO. 1120

DATE	ITEM	POST. REF.	DEBIT	CREDIT	BALANCE DEBIT	BALANCE CREDIT

ACCOUNT Accounts Receivable   ACCOUNT NO. 1125

DATE	ITEM	POST. REF.	DEBIT	CREDIT	BALANCE DEBIT	BALANCE CREDIT
20-- Dec. 1	Balance	✔			8 5 0 7 82	

ACCOUNT Allowance for Uncollectible Accounts   ACCOUNT NO. 1130

DATE	ITEM	POST. REF.	DEBIT	CREDIT	BALANCE DEBIT	BALANCE CREDIT
20-- Dec. 1	Balance	✔				4 2 60

1., 4., 5., 6., 9., 10., 11., 18., 19., 21.

GENERAL LEDGER

ACCOUNT Merchandise Inventory   ACCOUNT NO. 1135

DATE		ITEM	POST. REF.	DEBIT	CREDIT	BALANCE DEBIT	BALANCE CREDIT
20-- Dec.	1	Balance	✔			82 4 8 9 00	

ACCOUNT Supplies   ACCOUNT NO. 1140

DATE		ITEM	POST. REF.	DEBIT	CREDIT	BALANCE DEBIT	BALANCE CREDIT
20-- Dec.	1	Balance	✔			2 5 0 1 15	

ACCOUNT Prepaid Insurance   ACCOUNT NO. 1145

DATE		ITEM	POST. REF.	DEBIT	CREDIT	BALANCE DEBIT	BALANCE CREDIT
20-- Dec.	1	Balance	✔			8 6 0 0 00	

ACCOUNT Office Equipment   ACCOUNT NO. 1205

DATE		ITEM	POST. REF.	DEBIT	CREDIT	BALANCE DEBIT	BALANCE CREDIT
20-- Dec.	1	Balance	✔			23 4 8 0 00	

ACCOUNT Accumulated Depreciation—Office Equipment   ACCOUNT NO. 1210

DATE		ITEM	POST. REF.	DEBIT	CREDIT	BALANCE DEBIT	BALANCE CREDIT
20-- Dec.	1	Balance	✔				7 5 8 0 00

ACCOUNT Store Equipment   ACCOUNT NO. 1215

DATE		ITEM	POST. REF.	DEBIT	CREDIT	BALANCE DEBIT	BALANCE CREDIT
20-- Dec.	1	Balance	✔			29 0 1 0 00	

REINFORCEMENT ACTIVITY 3   PART A (continued)

1., 4., 5., 6., 9., 10., 11., 18., 19., 21.

GENERAL LEDGER

ACCOUNT Accumulated Depreciation—Store Equipment   ACCOUNT NO. 1220

DATE	ITEM	POST. REF.	DEBIT	CREDIT	BALANCE DEBIT	BALANCE CREDIT
20-- Dec. 1	Balance	✔				8 4 8 0 00

ACCOUNT Notes Payable   ACCOUNT NO. 2105

DATE	ITEM	POST. REF.	DEBIT	CREDIT	BALANCE DEBIT	BALANCE CREDIT
20-- Dec. 1	Balance	✔				20 0 0 0 00

ACCOUNT Interest Payable   ACCOUNT NO. 2110

DATE	ITEM	POST. REF.	DEBIT	CREDIT	BALANCE DEBIT	BALANCE CREDIT

ACCOUNT Accounts Payable   ACCOUNT NO. 2115

DATE	ITEM	POST. REF.	DEBIT	CREDIT	BALANCE DEBIT	BALANCE CREDIT
20-- Dec. 1	Balance	✔				20 0 9 2 10

ACCOUNT Employee Income Tax Payable   ACCOUNT NO. 2120

DATE	ITEM	POST. REF.	DEBIT	CREDIT	BALANCE DEBIT	BALANCE CREDIT
20-- Dec. 1	Balance	✔				2 1 2 5 00

ACCOUNT Federal Income Tax Payable   ACCOUNT NO. 2125

DATE	ITEM	POST. REF.	DEBIT	CREDIT	BALANCE DEBIT	BALANCE CREDIT

1., 4., 5., 6., 9., 10., 11., 18., 19., 21.

GENERAL LEDGER

ACCOUNT Social Security Tax Payable   ACCOUNT NO. 2130

DATE		ITEM	POST. REF.	DEBIT	CREDIT	BALANCE	
						DEBIT	CREDIT
Dec.	1	Balance	✔				1 1 5 0 00

ACCOUNT Medicare Tax Payable   ACCOUNT NO. 2135

DATE		ITEM	POST. REF.	DEBIT	CREDIT	BALANCE	
						DEBIT	CREDIT
Dec.	1	Balance	✔				2 6 5 40

ACCOUNT Sales Tax Payable   ACCOUNT NO. 2140

DATE		ITEM	POST. REF.	DEBIT	CREDIT	BALANCE	
						DEBIT	CREDIT
Dec.	1	Balance	✔				4 9 4 2 68

ACCOUNT Unemployment Tax Payable—Federal   ACCOUNT NO. 2145

DATE		ITEM	POST. REF.	DEBIT	CREDIT	BALANCE	
						DEBIT	CREDIT
Dec.	1	Balance	✔				1 3 05

ACCOUNT Unemployment Tax Payable—State   ACCOUNT NO. 2150

DATE		ITEM	POST. REF.	DEBIT	CREDIT	BALANCE	
						DEBIT	CREDIT
Dec.	1	Balance	✔				8 8 05

REINFORCEMENT ACTIVITY 3 PART A (continued)

1., 4., 5., 6., 9., 10., 11., 18., 19., 21.

GENERAL LEDGER

ACCOUNT Health Insurance Premiums Payable   ACCOUNT NO. 2155

DATE		ITEM	POST. REF.	DEBIT	CREDIT	BALANCE DEBIT	BALANCE CREDIT
20-- Dec.	1	Balance	✔				7 2 5 00

ACCOUNT Dividends Payable   ACCOUNT NO. 2160

DATE		ITEM	POST. REF.	DEBIT	CREDIT	BALANCE DEBIT	BALANCE CREDIT

ACCOUNT Capital Stock   ACCOUNT NO. 3105

DATE		ITEM	POST. REF.	DEBIT	CREDIT	BALANCE DEBIT	BALANCE CREDIT
20-- Dec.	1	Balance	✔				30 0 0 0 00

ACCOUNT Retained Earnings   ACCOUNT NO. 3110

DATE		ITEM	POST. REF.	DEBIT	CREDIT	BALANCE DEBIT	BALANCE CREDIT
20-- Dec.	1	Balance	✔				16 9 5 7 70

ACCOUNT Dividends   ACCOUNT NO. 3115

DATE		ITEM	POST. REF.	DEBIT	CREDIT	BALANCE DEBIT	BALANCE CREDIT
20-- Dec.	1	Balance	✔			20 0 0 0 00	

ACCOUNT Income Summary   ACCOUNT NO. 3120

DATE		ITEM	POST. REF.	DEBIT	CREDIT	BALANCE DEBIT	BALANCE CREDIT

1., 4., 5., 6., 9., 10., 11., 18., 19., 21.

GENERAL LEDGER

ACCOUNT Sales   ACCOUNT NO. 4105

DATE		ITEM	POST. REF.	DEBIT	CREDIT	BALANCE	
						DEBIT	CREDIT
Dec.	1	Balance	✔				756 3 9 7 90

ACCOUNT Sales Discount   ACCOUNT NO. 4110

DATE		ITEM	POST. REF.	DEBIT	CREDIT	BALANCE	
						DEBIT	CREDIT
Dec.	1	Balance	✔			1 8 7 8 60	

ACCOUNT Sales Returns and Allowances   ACCOUNT NO. 4115

DATE		ITEM	POST. REF.	DEBIT	CREDIT	BALANCE	
						DEBIT	CREDIT
Dec.	1	Balance	✔			6 0 5 4 80	

ACCOUNT Purchases   ACCOUNT NO. 5105

DATE		ITEM	POST. REF.	DEBIT	CREDIT	BALANCE	
						DEBIT	CREDIT
Dec.	1	Balance	✔			506 3 5 4 40	

ACCOUNT Purchases Discount   ACCOUNT NO. 5110

DATE		ITEM	POST. REF.	DEBIT	CREDIT	BALANCE	
						DEBIT	CREDIT
Dec.	1	Balance	✔				3 4 9 3 32

ACCOUNT Purchases Returns and Allowances   ACCOUNT NO. 5115

DATE		ITEM	POST. REF.	DEBIT	CREDIT	BALANCE	
						DEBIT	CREDIT
Dec.	1	Balance	✔				3 0 3 8 00

REINFORCEMENT ACTIVITY 3 PART A (continued)

1., 4., 5., 6., 9., 10., 11., 18., 19., 21.

GENERAL LEDGER

ACCOUNT Advertising Expense   ACCOUNT NO. 6105

DATE	ITEM	POST. REF.	DEBIT	CREDIT	BALANCE DEBIT	BALANCE CREDIT
20-- Dec. 1	Balance	✔			9 5 5 6 70	

ACCOUNT Cash Short and Over   ACCOUNT NO. 6110

DATE	ITEM	POST. REF.	DEBIT	CREDIT	BALANCE DEBIT	BALANCE CREDIT
20-- Dec. 1	Balance	✔			2 0 00	

ACCOUNT Credit Card Fee Expense   ACCOUNT NO. 6115

DATE	ITEM	POST. REF.	DEBIT	CREDIT	BALANCE DEBIT	BALANCE CREDIT
20-- Dec. 1	Balance	✔			14 1 1 1 40	

ACCOUNT Depreciation Expense—Office Equipment   ACCOUNT NO. 6120

DATE	ITEM	POST. REF.	DEBIT	CREDIT	BALANCE DEBIT	BALANCE CREDIT

ACCOUNT Depreciation Expense—Store Equipment   ACCOUNT NO. 6125

DATE	ITEM	POST. REF.	DEBIT	CREDIT	BALANCE DEBIT	BALANCE CREDIT

ACCOUNT Insurance Expense   ACCOUNT NO. 6130

DATE	ITEM	POST. REF.	DEBIT	CREDIT	BALANCE DEBIT	BALANCE CREDIT

1., 4., 5., 6., 9., 10., 11., 18., 19., 21.

GENERAL LEDGER

ACCOUNT Miscellaneous Expense   ACCOUNT NO. 6135

DATE	ITEM	POST. REF.	DEBIT	CREDIT	BALANCE DEBIT	BALANCE CREDIT
20-- Dec. 1	Balance	✔			5 7 3 3 95	

ACCOUNT Payroll Taxes Expense   ACCOUNT NO. 6140

DATE	ITEM	POST. REF.	DEBIT	CREDIT	BALANCE DEBIT	BALANCE CREDIT
20-- Dec. 1	Balance	✔			10 1 7 6 85	

ACCOUNT Rent Expense   ACCOUNT NO. 6145

DATE	ITEM	POST. REF.	DEBIT	CREDIT	BALANCE DEBIT	BALANCE CREDIT
20-- Dec. 1	Balance	✔			19 2 5 0 00	

ACCOUNT Repair Expense   ACCOUNT NO. 6150

DATE	ITEM	POST. REF.	DEBIT	CREDIT	BALANCE DEBIT	BALANCE CREDIT
20-- Dec. 1	Balance	✔			1 3 9 4 80	

ACCOUNT Salary Expense   ACCOUNT NO. 6155

DATE	ITEM	POST. REF.	DEBIT	CREDIT	BALANCE DEBIT	BALANCE CREDIT
20-- Dec. 1	Balance	✔			99 2 9 8 00	

REINFORCEMENT ACTIVITY 3   PART A (continued)

1., 4., 5., 6., 9., 10., 11., 18., 19., 21.

GENERAL LEDGER

ACCOUNT Supplies Expense   ACCOUNT NO. 6160

DATE	ITEM	POST. REF.	DEBIT	CREDIT	BALANCE DEBIT	BALANCE CREDIT

ACCOUNT Uncollectible Accounts Expense   ACCOUNT NO. 6165

DATE	ITEM	POST. REF.	DEBIT	CREDIT	BALANCE DEBIT	BALANCE CREDIT

ACCOUNT Utilities Expense   ACCOUNT NO. 6170

DATE	ITEM	POST. REF.	DEBIT	CREDIT	BALANCE DEBIT	BALANCE CREDIT
20-- Dec. 1	Balance	✔			6 8 9 0 00	

ACCOUNT Gain on Plant Assets   ACCOUNT NO. 7105

DATE	ITEM	POST. REF.	DEBIT	CREDIT	BALANCE DEBIT	BALANCE CREDIT
20-- Dec. 1	Balance	✔				3 6 5 00

ACCOUNT Interest Income   ACCOUNT NO. 7110

DATE	ITEM	POST. REF.	DEBIT	CREDIT	BALANCE DEBIT	BALANCE CREDIT
20-- Dec. 1	Balance	✔				1 8 0 00

ACCOUNT Interest Expense   ACCOUNT NO. 8105

DATE	ITEM	POST. REF.	DEBIT	CREDIT	BALANCE DEBIT	BALANCE CREDIT
20-- Dec. 1	Balance	✔			2 3 0 0 00	

1., 4., 5., 6., 9., 10., 11., 18., 19., 21.

GENERAL LEDGER

ACCOUNT Loss on Plant Assets   ACCOUNT NO. 8110

DATE		ITEM	POST. REF.	DEBIT	CREDIT	BALANCE DEBIT	BALANCE CREDIT
Dec.	1	Balance	✔			25000	

ACCOUNT Federal Income Tax Expense   ACCOUNT NO. 9105

DATE		ITEM	POST. REF.	DEBIT	CREDIT	BALANCE DEBIT	BALANCE CREDIT
Dec.	1	Balance	✔			1000000	

ACCOUNT   ACCOUNT NO.

DATE	ITEM	POST. REF.	DEBIT	CREDIT	BALANCE DEBIT	BALANCE CREDIT

ACCOUNT   ACCOUNT NO.

DATE	ITEM	POST. REF.	DEBIT	CREDIT	BALANCE DEBIT	BALANCE CREDIT

ACCOUNT   ACCOUNT NO.

DATE	ITEM	POST. REF.	DEBIT	CREDIT	BALANCE DEBIT	BALANCE CREDIT

REINFORCEMENT ACTIVITY 3 PART A (continued)

1., 4., 11.

ACCOUNTS RECEIVABLE LEDGER

CUSTOMER Jenni Baker   CUSTOMER NO. 110

DATE		ITEM	POST. REF.	DEBIT	CREDIT	DEBIT BALANCE
20-- Dec.	1	Balance	✔			1 3 5 0 00

CUSTOMER Patrick Felton   CUSTOMER NO. 120

DATE		ITEM	POST. REF.	DEBIT	CREDIT	DEBIT BALANCE
20-- Dec.	1	Balance	✔			1 6 7 9 48

CUSTOMER Hilldale Middle School   CUSTOMER NO. 130

DATE		ITEM	POST. REF.	DEBIT	CREDIT	DEBIT BALANCE

CUSTOMER Samuel Horton   CUSTOMER NO. 140

DATE		ITEM	POST. REF.	DEBIT	CREDIT	DEBIT BALANCE
20-- Dec.	1	Balance	✔			3 3 7 5 00

CUSTOMER Camille Nelson   CUSTOMER NO. 150

DATE		ITEM	POST. REF.	DEBIT	CREDIT	DEBIT BALANCE
20-- Dec.	1	Balance	✔			2 1 0 3 34

CUSTOMER Pam Ruocco   CUSTOMER NO. 160

DATE		ITEM	POST. REF.	DEBIT	CREDIT	DEBIT BALANCE

1., 4., 11.   **ACCOUNTS PAYABLE LEDGER**

VENDOR Buntin Supply Company   VENDOR NO. 210

DATE		ITEM	POST. REF.	DEBIT	CREDIT	CREDIT BALANCE
Dec.	1	Balance	✔			4 2 6 0 00

VENDOR Draper Company   VENDOR NO. 220

DATE		ITEM	POST. REF.	DEBIT	CREDIT	CREDIT BALANCE
Dec.	1	Balance	✔			5 4 3 7 00

VENDOR Glenson Company   VENDOR NO. 230

DATE		ITEM	POST. REF.	DEBIT	CREDIT	CREDIT BALANCE
Dec.	1	Balance	✔			2 7 8 4 70

VENDOR Hinsdale Supply Co.   VENDOR NO. 240

DATE		ITEM	POST. REF.	DEBIT	CREDIT	CREDIT BALANCE

VENDOR SHF Corp.   VENDOR NO. 250

DATE		ITEM	POST. REF.	DEBIT	CREDIT	CREDIT BALANCE
Dec.	1	Balance	✔			4 2 5 5 80

VENDOR Walbash Manufacturing   VENDOR NO. 260

DATE		ITEM	POST. REF.	DEBIT	CREDIT	CREDIT BALANCE
Dec.	1	Balance	✔			3 3 5 4 60

REINFORCEMENT ACTIVITY 3 **PART A (concluded)**

11.

20-1 WORK TOGETHER, p. 530

Estimating and journalizing entries for uncollectible accounts expense

6.

Velson Company

Work Sheet

For Year Ended December 31, 20 – –

	ACCOUNT TITLE	TRIAL BALANCE DEBIT	TRIAL BALANCE CREDIT	ADJUSTMENTS DEBIT	ADJUSTMENTS CREDIT
		1	2	3	4
6	Allowance for Uncollectible Accounts		8 5 3 00		
47	Uncollectible Accounts Expense				

7., 8.

GENERAL JOURNAL   PAGE 13

	DATE	ACCOUNT TITLE	DOC. NO.	POST. REF.	DEBIT	CREDIT	
1							1
2							2
3							3
4							4

8.   **GENERAL LEDGER**

ACCOUNT Accounts Receivable   ACCOUNT NO. 1125

DATE	ITEM	POST. REF.	DEBIT	CREDIT	BALANCE DEBIT	BALANCE CREDIT
20-- Dec. 31		S26	54 3 5 1 00		893 3 6 4 00	
31		CR24		45 6 8 4 00	847 6 8 0 00	

ACCOUNT Allowance for Uncollectible Accounts   ACCOUNT NO. 1130

DATE	ITEM	POST. REF.	DEBIT	CREDIT	BALANCE DEBIT	BALANCE CREDIT
20-- Dec. 28		G12	1 4 6 00			8 5 3 00

ACCOUNT Uncollectible Accounts Expense   ACCOUNT NO. 6165

DATE	ITEM	POST. REF.	DEBIT	CREDIT	BALANCE DEBIT	BALANCE CREDIT

Estimating and journalizing entries for uncollectible accounts expense

9.

McCain Company
Work Sheet
For Year Ended December 31, 20 – –

		1	2	3	4
	ACCOUNT TITLE	TRIAL BALANCE		ADJUSTMENTS	
		DEBIT	CREDIT	DEBIT	CREDIT
6	Allowance for Uncollectible Accounts		1 4 5 00		
47	Uncollectible Accounts Expense				

10., 11.

GENERAL JOURNAL
PAGE 18

	DATE	ACCOUNT TITLE	DOC. NO.	POST. REF.	DEBIT	CREDIT	
1							1
2							2
3							3
4							4

11.

GENERAL LEDGER

ACCOUNT Accounts Receivable ACCOUNT NO. 1125

DATE	ITEM	POST. REF.	DEBIT	CREDIT	BALANCE DEBIT	BALANCE CREDIT
20-- Dec. 31		S18	40 2 4 5 00		154 8 1 8 00	
31		CR16		34 5 0 2 00	120 3 1 6 00	

ACCOUNT Allowance for Uncollectible Accounts ACCOUNT NO. 1130

DATE	ITEM	POST. REF.	DEBIT	CREDIT	BALANCE DEBIT	BALANCE CREDIT
20-- Dec. 22		G12	3 2 6 00			1 4 5 00

ACCOUNT Uncollectible Accounts Expense ACCOUNT NO. 6165

DATE	ITEM	POST. REF.	DEBIT	CREDIT	BALANCE DEBIT	BALANCE CREDIT

20-2 **WORK TOGETHER, p. 536**

Recording entries relating to uncollectible accounts receivable

4., 5., 6.

GENERAL JOURNAL   PAGE 6

	DATE	ACCOUNT TITLE	DOC. NO.	POST. REF.	DEBIT	CREDIT	
1							1
2							2
3							3
4							4
5							5
6							6
7							7
8							8
9							9
10							10
11							11
12							12

4., 5.

CASH RECEIPTS JOURNAL   PAGE 9

	DATE	ACCOUNT TITLE	DOC. NO.	POST. REF.	GENERAL DEBIT	GENERAL CREDIT	ACCOUNTS RECEIVABLE CREDIT	SALES CREDIT	SALES TAX PAYABLE DEBIT	SALES TAX PAYABLE CREDIT	SALES DISCOUNT DEBIT	CASH DEBIT
					1	2	3	4	5	6	7	8
1												
2												
3												
4												
5												

Recording entries relating to uncollectible accounts receivable

7., 8., 9.

GENERAL JOURNAL

PAGE 11

DATE	ACCOUNT TITLE	DOC. NO.	POST. REF.	DEBIT	CREDIT	
						1
						2
						3
						4
						5
						6
						7
						8
						9
						10
						11
						12

7., 8.

CASH RECEIPTS JOURNAL

PAGE 15

DATE	ACCOUNT TITLE	DOC. NO.	POST. REF.	GENERAL DEBIT	GENERAL CREDIT	ACCOUNTS RECEIVABLE CREDIT	SALES CREDIT	SALES TAX PAYABLE DEBIT	SALES TAX PAYABLE CREDIT	SALES DISCOUNT DEBIT	CASH DEBIT	
												1
												2
												3
												4
												5

20-2 **WORK TOGETHER (continued)**

6.

GENERAL LEDGER

ACCOUNT Accounts Receivable   ACCOUNT NO. 1125

DATE	ITEM	POST. REF.	DEBIT	CREDIT	BALANCE DEBIT	BALANCE CREDIT
20-- June 1	Balance	✔			62 45 8 00	

ACCOUNT Allowance for Uncollectible Accounts   ACCOUNT NO. 1130

DATE	ITEM	POST. REF.	DEBIT	CREDIT	BALANCE DEBIT	BALANCE CREDIT
20-- June 1	Balance	✔				8 45 8 00

ACCOUNT Uncollectible Accounts Expense   ACCOUNT NO. 6165

DATE	ITEM	POST. REF.	DEBIT	CREDIT	BALANCE DEBIT	BALANCE CREDIT

ACCOUNT   ACCOUNT NO.

DATE	ITEM	POST. REF.	DEBIT	CREDIT	BALANCE DEBIT	BALANCE CREDIT

ACCOUNT   ACCOUNT NO.

DATE	ITEM	POST. REF.	DEBIT	CREDIT	BALANCE DEBIT	BALANCE CREDIT

5.

ACCOUNTS RECEIVABLE LEDGER

CUSTOMER Johnston, Inc.   CUSTOMER NO. 110

DATE	ITEM	POST. REF.	DEBIT	CREDIT	DEBIT BALANCE
20-- Jan. 5		S1	8 1 9 00		8 1 9 00

CUSTOMER Kelton Corporation   CUSTOMER NO. 120

DATE	ITEM	POST. REF.	DEBIT	CREDIT	DEBIT BALANCE
20-- Mar. 2		S3	3 9 6 00		3 9 6 00

CUSTOMER Marris, Inc.   CUSTOMER NO. 130

DATE	ITEM	POST. REF.	DEBIT	CREDIT	DEBIT BALANCE
20-- Feb. 14	Written off	G2		5 7 1 00	—

CUSTOMER Matlin Co.   CUSTOMER NO. 140

DATE	ITEM	POST. REF.	DEBIT	CREDIT	DEBIT BALANCE
20-- Mar. 4		S3	5 7 5 00		5 7 5 00

CUSTOMER   CUSTOMER NO.

DATE	ITEM	POST. REF.	DEBIT	CREDIT	DEBIT BALANCE

20-2 ON YOUR OWN (continued)

9.

GENERAL LEDGER

ACCOUNT Accounts Receivable   ACCOUNT NO. 1125

DATE		ITEM	POST. REF.	DEBIT	CREDIT	BALANCE	
						DEBIT	CREDIT
20-- Nov.	1	Balance	✔			50 1 4 8 00	

ACCOUNT Allowance for Uncollectible Accounts   ACCOUNT NO. 1130

DATE		ITEM	POST. REF.	DEBIT	CREDIT	BALANCE	
						DEBIT	CREDIT
20-- Nov.	1	Balance	✔				3 4 5 8 00

ACCOUNT Uncollectible Accounts Expense   ACCOUNT NO. 6165

DATE		ITEM	POST. REF.	DEBIT	CREDIT	BALANCE	
						DEBIT	CREDIT

ACCOUNT   ACCOUNT NO.

DATE		ITEM	POST. REF.	DEBIT	CREDIT	BALANCE	
						DEBIT	CREDIT

ACCOUNT   ACCOUNT NO.

DATE		ITEM	POST. REF.	DEBIT	CREDIT	BALANCE	
						DEBIT	CREDIT

8.

ACCOUNTS RECEIVABLE LEDGER

CUSTOMER Peter Ewing   CUSTOMER NO. 110

DATE	ITEM	POST. REF.	DEBIT	CREDIT	DEBIT BALANCE
20-- Jan. 9		S1	6 1 2 00		6 1 2 00

CUSTOMER Tim Haley   CUSTOMER NO. 120

DATE	ITEM	POST. REF.	DEBIT	CREDIT	DEBIT BALANCE
20-- Mar. 13		S3	2 3 8 00		2 3 8 00

CUSTOMER Mike Novak   CUSTOMER NO. 130

DATE	ITEM	POST. REF.	DEBIT	CREDIT	DEBIT BALANCE
20-- Apr. 6	Written off	G4		8 5 3 00	— —

CUSTOMER Angela White   CUSTOMER NO. 140

DATE	ITEM	POST. REF.	DEBIT	CREDIT	DEBIT BALANCE
20-- Feb. 23		S2	1 5 9 00		1 5 9 00

CUSTOMER   CUSTOMER NO.

DATE	ITEM	POST. REF.	DEBIT	CREDIT	DEBIT BALANCE

Name _____ Date _____ Class _____

20-1 APPLICATION PROBLEM, p. 538

Estimating and journalizing entries for uncollectible accounts expense

1.

Kellogg, Inc.

Work Sheet

For Year Ended December 31, 20 – –

	ACCOUNT TITLE	TRIAL BALANCE		ADJUSTMENTS	
		DEBIT	CREDIT	DEBIT	CREDIT
6	Allowance for Uncollectible Accounts		53400		
47	Uncollectible Accounts Expense				

2., 3.

GENERAL JOURNAL   PAGE 25

	DATE	ACCOUNT TITLE	DOC. NO.	POST. REF.	DEBIT	CREDIT	
1							1
2							2
3							3
4							4

3.   **GENERAL LEDGER**

ACCOUNT Accounts Receivable   ACCOUNT NO. 1125

DATE	ITEM	POST. REF.	DEBIT	CREDIT	BALANCE DEBIT	BALANCE CREDIT
20-- Dec. 31		S22	618 42 00		105 483 00	
31		CR24		748 48 00	30 635 00	

ACCOUNT Allowance for Uncollectible Accounts   ACCOUNT NO. 1130

DATE	ITEM	POST. REF.	DEBIT	CREDIT	BALANCE DEBIT	BALANCE CREDIT
20-- Dec. 28		G24	16 48 00			53400

ACCOUNT Uncollectible Accounts Expense   ACCOUNT NO. 6165

DATE	ITEM	POST. REF.	DEBIT	CREDIT	BALANCE DEBIT	BALANCE CREDIT

Extra form

GENERAL JOURNAL   PAGE

	DATE	ACCOUNT TITLE	DOC. NO.	POST. REF.	DEBIT	CREDIT	
1							1
2							2
3							3
4							4
5							5
6							6
7							7
8							8
9							9
10							10
11							11
12							12
13							13
14							14
15							15
16							16
17							17
18							18
19							19
20							20
21							21
22							22
23							23
24							24
25							25
26							26
27							27
28							28
29							29
30							30
31							31
32							32
33							33

20-2 APPLICATION PROBLEM, p. 538

Recording entries related to uncollectible accounts receivable

1., 2., 3.

GENERAL JOURNAL

PAGE 7

	DATE		ACCOUNT TITLE	DOC. NO.	POST. REF.	DEBIT	CREDIT	
1								1
2								2
3								3
4								4
5								5
6								6
7								7
8								8
9								9
10								10
11								11
12								12
13								13
14								14
15								15
16								16
17								17
18								18
19								19
20								20
21								21
22								22
23								23
24								24
25								25
26								26
27								27
28								28
29								29
30								30
31								31
32								32

1., 2.

CASH RECEIPTS JOURNAL

PAGE 9

	DATE	ACCOUNT TITLE	DOC. NO.	POST. REF.	GENERAL		ACCOUNTS RECEIVABLE CREDIT	SALES CREDIT	SALES TAX PAYABLE		SALES DISCOUNT DEBIT	CASH DEBIT
					DEBIT	CREDIT			DEBIT	CREDIT		
					1	2	3	4	5	6	7	8
1												
2												
3												
4												
5												
6												
7												
8												
9												
10												
11												
12												
13												
14												
15												
16												
17												
18												
19												
20												
21												
22												
23												

20-2 APPLICATION PROBLEM (continued)

3.

GENERAL LEDGER

ACCOUNT Accounts Receivable   ACCOUNT NO. 1125

DATE		ITEM	POST. REF.	DEBIT	CREDIT	BALANCE DEBIT	BALANCE CREDIT
20-- July	1	Balance	✔			24 854 00	

ACCOUNT Allowance for Uncollectible Accounts   ACCOUNT NO. 1130

DATE		ITEM	POST. REF.	DEBIT	CREDIT	BALANCE DEBIT	BALANCE CREDIT
20-- July	1	Balance	✔				3 075 00

ACCOUNT Uncollectible Accounts Expense   ACCOUNT NO. 6165

DATE		ITEM	POST. REF.	DEBIT	CREDIT	BALANCE DEBIT	BALANCE CREDIT

ACCOUNT   ACCOUNT NO.

DATE		ITEM	POST. REF.	DEBIT	CREDIT	BALANCE DEBIT	BALANCE CREDIT

ACCOUNT   ACCOUNT NO.

DATE		ITEM	POST. REF.	DEBIT	CREDIT	BALANCE DEBIT	BALANCE CREDIT

2.

ACCOUNTS RECEIVABLE LEDGER

CUSTOMER David Dowdle   CUSTOMER NO. 110

DATE		ITEM	POST. REF.	DEBIT	CREDIT	DEBIT BALANCE
Jan. 20--	26	Written off	G1		1 5 7 00	—

CUSTOMER Annie Jamison   CUSTOMER NO. 120

DATE		ITEM	POST. REF.	DEBIT	CREDIT	DEBIT BALANCE
Jan. 20--	3		S1	1 0 2 00		1 0 2 00

CUSTOMER Jeanne Lewis   CUSTOMER NO. 130

DATE		ITEM	POST. REF.	DEBIT	CREDIT	DEBIT BALANCE
Feb. 20--	2		S2	9 7 00		9 7 00

CUSTOMER Rebecca Snow   CUSTOMER NO. 140

DATE		ITEM	POST. REF.	DEBIT	CREDIT	DEBIT BALANCE
Mar. 20--	4		S3	3 1 0 00		3 1 0 00

CUSTOMER   CUSTOMER NO.

DATE	ITEM	POST. REF.	DEBIT	CREDIT	DEBIT BALANCE

20-3 APPLICATION PROBLEM, p. 538

Recording entries related to uncollectible accounts receivable

1., 2., 3.

GENERAL JOURNAL   PAGE 4

	DATE	ACCOUNT TITLE	DOC. NO.	POST. REF.	DEBIT	CREDIT	
1							1
2							2
3							3
4							4
5							5
6							6
7							7
8							8
9							9
10							10
11							11
12							12
13							13
14							14
15							15
16							16
17							17
18							18
19							19
20							20
21							21
22							22
23							23
24							24
25							25
26							26
27							27
28							28
29							29
30							30
31							31
32							32

1., 2.

CASH RECEIPTS JOURNAL

PAGE 2

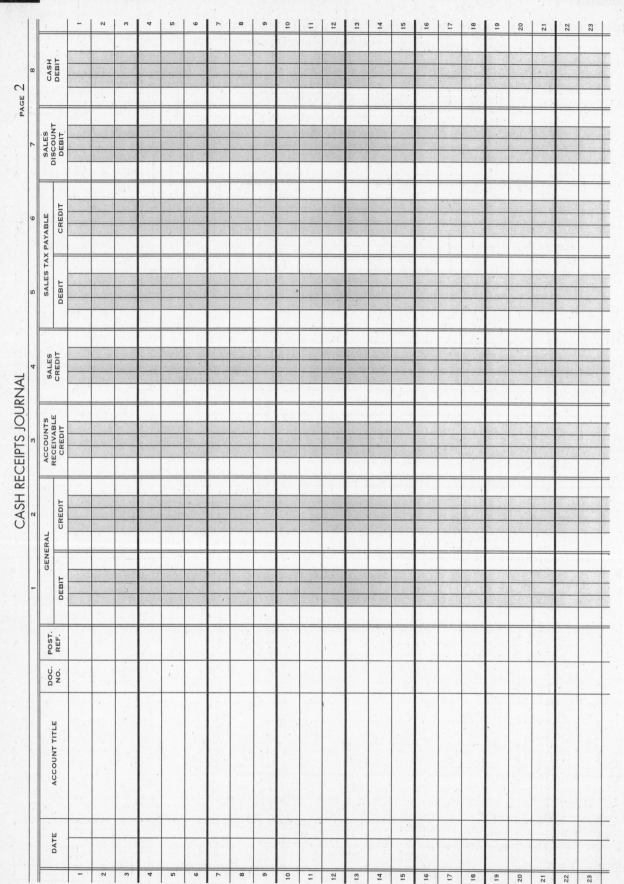

	DATE	ACCOUNT TITLE	DOC. NO.	POST. REF.	GENERAL DEBIT	GENERAL CREDIT	ACCOUNTS RECEIVABLE CREDIT	SALES CREDIT	SALES TAX PAYABLE DEBIT	SALES TAX PAYABLE CREDIT	SALES DISCOUNT DEBIT	CASH DEBIT	
					1	2	3	4	5	6	7	8	
1													1
2													2
3													3
4													4
5													5
6													6
7													7
8													8
9													9
10													10
11													11
12													12
13													13
14													14
15													15
16													16
17													17
18													18
19													19
20													20
21													21
22													22
23													23

20-3 **APPLICATION PROBLEM (continued)**

3.

GENERAL LEDGER

ACCOUNT Accounts Receivable   ACCOUNT NO. 1125

DATE		ITEM	POST. REF.	DEBIT	CREDIT	BALANCE	
						DEBIT	CREDIT
20-- Feb.	1	Balance	✔			54 15 8 00	

ACCOUNT Allowance for Uncollectible Accounts   ACCOUNT NO. 1130

DATE		ITEM	POST. REF.	DEBIT	CREDIT	BALANCE	
						DEBIT	CREDIT
20-- Feb.	1	Balance	✔				9 15 4 00

ACCOUNT Uncollectible Accounts Expense   ACCOUNT NO. 6165

DATE		ITEM	POST. REF.	DEBIT	CREDIT	BALANCE	
						DEBIT	CREDIT

ACCOUNT   ACCOUNT NO.

DATE		ITEM	POST. REF.	DEBIT	CREDIT	BALANCE	
						DEBIT	CREDIT

ACCOUNT   ACCOUNT NO.

DATE		ITEM	POST. REF.	DEBIT	CREDIT	BALANCE	
						DEBIT	CREDIT

2.

ACCOUNTS RECEIVABLE LEDGER

CUSTOMER Bearden Co.   CUSTOMER NO. 110

DATE		ITEM	POST. REF.	DEBIT	CREDIT	DEBIT BALANCE
20-- Jan.	3	Written off	G1		1 4 5 8 00	—

CUSTOMER Camden Enterprises   CUSTOMER NO. 120

DATE		ITEM	POST. REF.	DEBIT	CREDIT	DEBIT BALANCE
20-- Jan.	3	Written off	G1		1 7 8 4 00	—

CUSTOMER Hampton Industries   CUSTOMER NO. 130

DATE		ITEM	POST. REF.	DEBIT	CREDIT	DEBIT BALANCE
20-- Jan.	1	Balance	✔			2 5 8 4 00

CUSTOMER Rankin Co.   CUSTOMER NO. 140

DATE		ITEM	POST. REF.	DEBIT	CREDIT	DEBIT BALANCE
20-- Jan.	1	Balance	✔			9 4 8 00

CUSTOMER Wilmont Co.   CUSTOMER NO. 150

DATE		ITEM	POST. REF.	DEBIT	CREDIT	DEBIT BALANCE
20-- Jan.	1	Balance	✔			5 4 8 00

20-4 MASTERY PROBLEM, p. 539

Recording entries for uncollectible accounts

1.

GENERAL JOURNAL   PAGE 10

	DATE	ACCOUNT TITLE	DOC. NO.	POST. REF.	DEBIT	CREDIT	
1							1
2							2
3							3
4							4

2.

GENERAL JOURNAL   PAGE 11

	DATE	ACCOUNT TITLE	DOC. NO.	POST. REF.	DEBIT	CREDIT	
1							1
2							2
3							3
4							4
5							5
6							6

3.

GENERAL JOURNAL   PAGE 12

	DATE	ACCOUNT TITLE	DOC. NO.	POST. REF.	DEBIT	CREDIT	
1							1
2							2
3							3
4							4
5							5
6							6

4.

GENERAL JOURNAL   PAGE 13

	DATE	ACCOUNT TITLE	DOC. NO.	POST. REF.	DEBIT	CREDIT	
1							1
2							2
3							3

2.

CASH RECEIPTS JOURNAL

PAGE 11

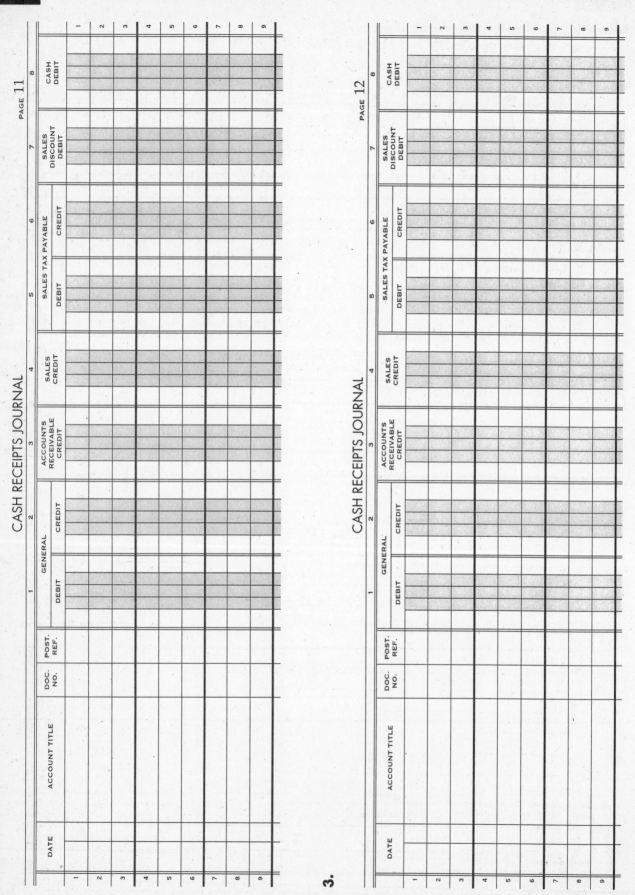

3.

CASH RECEIPTS JOURNAL

PAGE 12

20-4 MASTERY PROBLEM (continued)

1., 2., 3., 4.

GENERAL LEDGER

ACCOUNT Cash   ACCOUNT NO. 1105

DATE	ITEM	POST. REF.	DEBIT	CREDIT	BALANCE DEBIT	BALANCE CREDIT
20-- Oct. 1	Balance	✔			5 0 4 8 00	

ACCOUNT Accounts Receivable   ACCOUNT NO. 1125

DATE	ITEM	POST. REF.	DEBIT	CREDIT	BALANCE DEBIT	BALANCE CREDIT
20-- Oct. 1	Balance	✔			64 5 8 7 00	

ACCOUNT Allowance for Uncollectible Accounts   ACCOUNT NO. 1130

DATE	ITEM	POST. REF.	DEBIT	CREDIT	BALANCE DEBIT	BALANCE CREDIT
20-- Oct. 1	Balance	✔				1 5 4 8 20

ACCOUNT Uncollectible Accounts Expense   ACCOUNT NO. 6165

DATE	ITEM	POST. REF.	DEBIT	CREDIT	BALANCE DEBIT	BALANCE CREDIT

1., 2., 3.

ACCOUNTS RECEIVABLE LEDGER

CUSTOMER Burrell Company   CUSTOMER NO. 125

DATE	ITEM	POST. REF.	DEBIT	CREDIT	DEBIT BALANCE
20-- Mar. 28		S3	7 1 4 15		7 1 4 15

CUSTOMER Fiber-Tech   CUSTOMER NO. 135

DATE	ITEM	POST. REF.	DEBIT	CREDIT	DEBIT BALANCE
20-- Mar. 15		S3	8 2 9 35		8 2 9 35

CUSTOMER Gentry Corporation   CUSTOMER NO. 140

DATE	ITEM	POST. REF.	DEBIT	CREDIT	DEBIT BALANCE
20-- Jan. 16		S1	4 8 2 50		4 8 2 50

CUSTOMER Kingston Corporation   CUSTOMER NO. 150

DATE	ITEM	POST. REF.	DEBIT	CREDIT	DEBIT BALANCE
20-- Feb. 4		S2	2 4 7 60		2 4 7 60

CUSTOMER Peterson, Inc.   CUSTOMER NO. 160

DATE	ITEM	POST. REF.	DEBIT	CREDIT	DEBIT BALANCE
20-- Mar. 4	Written off	G3		5 2 3 30	—

20-5 CHALLENGE PROBLEM, p. 540

Recording entries for uncollectible accounts

Extra form

21-1 WORK TOGETHER, p. 548

Journalizing buying plant assets and paying property tax

5., 6.

CASH PAYMENTS JOURNAL

PAGE 1

DATE	ACCOUNT TITLE	CK. NO.	POST. REF.	GENERAL DEBIT	GENERAL CREDIT	ACCOUNTS PAYABLE DEBIT	PURCHASES DISCOUNT CREDIT	CASH CREDIT

GENERAL LEDGER

6.

ACCOUNT Office Equipment   ACCOUNT NO. 1205

DATE	ITEM	POST. REF.	DEBIT	CREDIT	BALANCE DEBIT	BALANCE CREDIT
20-- Jan. 1	Balance	✓			25 4 8 0 00	

ACCOUNT Store Equipment   ACCOUNT NO. 1215

DATE	ITEM	POST. REF.	DEBIT	CREDIT	BALANCE DEBIT	BALANCE CREDIT
20-- Jan. 1	Balance	✓			15 4 8 0 00	

ACCOUNT Property Tax Expense   ACCOUNT NO. 6142

DATE	ITEM	POST. REF.	DEBIT	CREDIT	BALANCE DEBIT	BALANCE CREDIT

Journalizing buying plant assets and paying property tax

7., 8.

CASH PAYMENTS JOURNAL

PAGE 1

DATE	ACCOUNT TITLE	CK. NO.	POST. REF.	1 GENERAL DEBIT	2 GENERAL CREDIT	3 ACCOUNTS PAYABLE DEBIT	4 PURCHASES DISCOUNT CREDIT	5 CASH CREDIT

GENERAL LEDGER

8.

ACCOUNT Office Equipment   ACCOUNT NO. 1205

DATE	ITEM	POST. REF.	DEBIT	CREDIT	BALANCE DEBIT	BALANCE CREDIT
20-- Jan.	1	Balance	✓			15 4 8 0 00	

ACCOUNT Store Equipment   ACCOUNT NO. 1215

DATE	ITEM	POST. REF.	DEBIT	CREDIT	BALANCE DEBIT	BALANCE CREDIT
20-- Jan.	1	Balance	✓			9 7 3 0 00	

ACCOUNT Property Tax Expense   ACCOUNT NO. 6142

DATE	ITEM	POST. REF.	DEBIT	CREDIT	BALANCE DEBIT	BALANCE CREDIT

21-2 WORK TOGETHER, p. 552

Calculating depreciation

Plant asset: _____   Original cost: _____
Depreciation method: _____   Estimated salvage value: _____
Estimated useful life: _____

Year	Beginning Book Value	Annual Depreciation	Accumulated Depreciation	Ending Book Value

Plant asset: _____   Original cost: _____
Depreciation method: _____   Estimated salvage value: _____
Estimated useful life: _____

Year	Beginning Book Value	Annual Depreciation	Accumulated Depreciation	Ending Book Value

Calculating depreciation

Plant asset: _____ Original cost: _____

Depreciation method: _____ Estimated salvage value: _____

Estimated useful life: _____

Year	Beginning Book Value	Annual Depreciation	Accumulated Depreciation	Ending Book Value

Plant asset: _____ Original cost: _____

Depreciation method: _____ Estimated salvage value: _____

Estimated useful life: _____

Year	Beginning Book Value	Annual Depreciation	Accumulated Depreciation	Ending Book Value

21-3 and 21-4 WORK TOGETHER, pp. 556, 561

21-3 Journalizing depreciation
21-4 Recording the disposal of plant assets

3., 7.

PLANT ASSET RECORD No. ____   General Ledger Account No. _____

Description _____   General Ledger Account _____

Date   Serial
Bought _____   Number _____   Original Cost _____

                              Estimated
Estimated   Salvage   Depreciation
Useful Life _____   Value _____   Method _____

Disposed of: Discarded _____   Sold _____   Traded _____
Date _____   Disposal Amount _____

Year	Annual Depreciation Expense	Accumulated Depreciation	Ending Book Value

Continue record on back of card

21-3 Journalizing depreciation
21-4 Recording the disposal of plant assets

5., 10.

PLANT ASSET RECORD No. _____   General Ledger Account No. _____

Description _____   General Ledger Account _____

Date   Serial
Bought _____   Number _____   Original Cost _____

                               Estimated
Estimated   Salvage   Depreciation
Useful Life _____   Value _____   Method _____

Disposed of: Discarded _____   Sold _____   Traded _____
Date _____   Disposal Amount _____

Year	Annual Depreciation Expense	Accumulated Depreciation	Ending Book Value

Continue record on back of card

21-3 and 21-4 **WORK TOGETHER (continued)**

3., 7.

PLANT ASSET RECORD No. ____		General Ledger Account No. _____

Description _____   General Ledger Account _____

Date
Bought _____   Serial
Number _____   Original Cost _____

Estimated
Useful Life _____   Estimated
Salvage
Value _____   Depreciation
Method _____

Disposed of: Discarded _____   Sold _____   Traded _____
Date _____   Disposal Amount _____

Year	Annual Depreciation Expense	Accumulated Depreciation	Ending Book Value
	Continue record on back of card		

5., 10.

PLANT ASSET RECORD No. _____		General Ledger Account No. _____	
Description _____		General Ledger Account \ _____	
Date Bought _____	Serial Number _____	Original Cost _____	
Estimated Useful Life _____	Estimated Salvage Value _____	Depreciation Method _____	

Disposed of: Date _____	Discarded _____	Sold _____	Traded _____
		Disposal Amount _____	

Year	Annual Depreciation Expense	Accumulated Depreciation	Ending Book Value

Continue record on back of card

21-3 WORK TOGETHER (concluded)

4.

Gabriel, Inc.

Work Sheet

For Year Ended December 31, 20 – –

	ACCOUNT TITLE	TRIAL BALANCE		ADJUSTMENTS	
		DEBIT	CREDIT	DEBIT	CREDIT
10	Office Equipment	24 5 8 7 00			
11	Accumulated Depreciation—Office Equipment		8 4 5 4 00		
38	Depreciation Expense—Office Equipment				

GENERAL JOURNAL
PAGE 18

	DATE	ACCOUNT TITLE	DOC. NO.	POST. REF.	DEBIT	CREDIT	
1							1
2							2
3							3
4							4

GENERAL LEDGER

ACCOUNT Office Equipment   ACCOUNT NO. 1205

DATE	ITEM	POST. REF.	DEBIT	CREDIT	BALANCE DEBIT	BALANCE CREDIT
20-- Dec. 31	Balance	✔			24 5 8 7 00	

ACCOUNT Accumulated Depreciation—Office Equipment   ACCOUNT NO. 1210

DATE	ITEM	POST. REF.	DEBIT	CREDIT	BALANCE DEBIT	BALANCE CREDIT
20-- Jan. 1	Balance	✔				8 4 5 4 00

ACCOUNT Depreciation Expense—Office Equipment   ACCOUNT NO. 6120

DATE	ITEM	POST. REF.	DEBIT	CREDIT	BALANCE DEBIT	BALANCE CREDIT

6.

Yeatman Co.

Work Sheet

For Year Ended December 31, 20 – –

	1		2		3		4	
	TRIAL BALANCE				ADJUSTMENTS			
ACCOUNT TITLE	DEBIT		CREDIT		DEBIT		CREDIT	
12 Store Equipment	54 8 7 8 00							
13 Accumulated Depreciation—Store Equipment			24 5 8 0 00					
39 Depreciation Expense—Store Equipment								

GENERAL JOURNAL   PAGE 13

	DATE	ACCOUNT TITLE	DOC. NO.	POST. REF.	DEBIT	CREDIT	
1							1
2							2
3							3
4							4

GENERAL LEDGER

ACCOUNT Store Equipment   ACCOUNT NO. 1215

DATE	ITEM	POST. REF.	DEBIT	CREDIT	BALANCE DEBIT	BALANCE CREDIT
20-- Dec. 31	Balance	✔			54 8 7 8 00	

ACCOUNT Accumulated Depreciation—Store Equipment   ACCOUNT NO. 1220

DATE	ITEM	POST. REF.	DEBIT	CREDIT	BALANCE DEBIT	BALANCE CREDIT
20-- Jan. 1	Balance	✔				24 5 8 0 00

ACCOUNT Depreciation Expense—Store Equipment   ACCOUNT NO. 6125

DATE	ITEM	POST. REF.	DEBIT	CREDIT	BALANCE DEBIT	BALANCE CREDIT

21-4 **WORK TOGETHER (concluded)**

5.

GENERAL JOURNAL

PAGE 3

DATE	ACCOUNT TITLE	DOC. NO.	POST. REF.	DEBIT	CREDIT	
						1
						2
						3
						4
						5
						6

6.

CASH RECEIPTS JOURNAL

PAGE 3

				1	2	3	4	5	6	7	8
DATE	ACCOUNT TITLE	DOC. NO.	POST. REF.	GENERAL DEBIT	GENERAL CREDIT	ACCOUNTS RECEIVABLE CREDIT	SALES CREDIT	SALES TAX PAYABLE DEBIT	SALES TAX PAYABLE CREDIT	SALES DISCOUNT DEBIT	CASH DEBIT

8.

GENERAL JOURNAL

PAGE 4

DATE	ACCOUNT TITLE	DOC. NO.	POST. REF.	DEBIT	CREDIT

9.

CASH RECEIPTS JOURNAL

PAGE 1

				GENERAL		ACCOUNTS RECEIVABLE CREDIT	SALES CREDIT	SALES TAX PAYABLE		SALES DISCOUNT DEBIT	CASH DEBIT
DATE	ACCOUNT TITLE	DOC. NO.	POST. REF.	DEBIT	CREDIT			DEBIT	CREDIT		

21-5 WORK TOGETHER, p. 565

Calculating depreciation using the double declining-balance depreciation method

Plant asset: _____   Original cost: _____

Depreciation method: _____   Estimated salvage value: _____

Estimated useful life: _____

Year	Beginning Book Value	Declining-Balance Rate	Annual Depreciation	Ending Book Value
1				
2				
3				
4				
5				
6				
7				

Plant asset: _____   Original cost: _____

Depreciation method: _____   Estimated salvage value: _____

Estimated useful life: _____

Year	Beginning Book Value	Declining-Balance Rate	Annual Depreciation	Ending Book Value
1				
2				
3				
4				
5				
6				
7				

Plant asset: _____   Original cost: _____

Depreciation method: _____   Estimated salvage value: _____

Estimated useful life: _____

Year	Beginning Book Value	Declining-Balance Rate	Annual Depreciation	Ending Book Value
1				
2				
3				
4				
5				
6				
7				

Calculating depreciation using the double declining-balance depreciation method

Plant asset: _____ Original cost: _____

Depreciation method: _____ Estimated salvage value: _____

Estimated useful life: _____

Year	Beginning Book Value	Declining-Balance Rate	Annual Depreciation	Ending Book Value
1				
2				
3				
4				
5				
6				
7				

Plant asset: _____ Original cost: _____

Depreciation method: _____ Estimated salvage value: _____

Estimated useful life: _____

Year	Beginning Book Value	Declining-Balance Rate	Annual Depreciation	Ending Book Value
1				
2				
3				
4				
5				
6				
7				

Plant asset: _____ Original cost: _____

Depreciation method: _____ Estimated salvage value: _____

Estimated useful life: _____

Year	Beginning Book Value	Declining-Balance Rate	Annual Depreciation	Ending Book Value
1				
2				
3				
4				
5				
6				
7				
8				

21-1 **APPLICATION PROBLEM, p. 567**

Journalizing buying plant assets and paying property tax

1., 2.

CASH PAYMENTS JOURNAL

PAGE 1

DATE	ACCOUNT TITLE	CK. NO.	POST. REF.	GENERAL DEBIT	GENERAL CREDIT	ACCOUNTS PAYABLE DEBIT	PURCHASES DISCOUNT CREDIT	CASH CREDIT

2.

GENERAL LEDGER

ACCOUNT Office Equipment   ACCOUNT NO. 1205

DATE	ITEM	POST. REF.	DEBIT	CREDIT	BALANCE DEBIT	BALANCE CREDIT
20-- Jan. 1	Balance	✓			24 150 00	

ACCOUNT Store Equipment   ACCOUNT NO. 1215

DATE	ITEM	POST. REF.	DEBIT	CREDIT	BALANCE DEBIT	BALANCE CREDIT
20-- Jan. 1	Balance	✓			15 470 00	

ACCOUNT Property Tax Expense   ACCOUNT NO. 6142

DATE	ITEM	POST. REF.	DEBIT	CREDIT	BALANCE DEBIT	BALANCE CREDIT

Extra form

CASH PAYMENTS JOURNAL

PAGE

				GENERAL		ACCOUNTS PAYABLE DEBIT	PURCHASES DISCOUNT CREDIT	CASH CREDIT
DATE	ACCOUNT TITLE	CK. NO.	POST. REF.	DEBIT	CREDIT			

21-2 APPLICATION PROBLEM, p. 567

Calculating depreciation

Plant asset: _____   Original cost: _____
Depreciation method: _____   Estimated salvage value: _____
                                        Estimated useful life: _____

Year	Beginning Book Value	Annual Depreciation	Accumulated Depreciation	Ending Book Value

Plant asset: _____   Original cost: _____
Depreciation method: _____   Estimated salvage value: _____
                                        Estimated useful life: _____

Year	Beginning Book Value	Annual Depreciation	Accumulated Depreciation	Ending Book Value

Plant asset: _____   Original cost: _____
Depreciation method: _____   Estimated salvage value: _____
                                        Estimated useful life: _____

Year	Beginning Book Value	Annual Depreciation	Accumulated Depreciation	Ending Book Value

Extra forms

Plant asset:		Original cost:	
Depreciation method:		Estimated salvage value:	
		Estimated useful life:	

Year	Beginning Book Value	Annual Depreciation	Accumulated Depreciation	Ending Book Value

Plant asset:		Original cost:	
Depreciation method:		Estimated salvage value:	
		Estimated useful life:	

Year	Beginning Book Value	Annual Depreciation	Accumulated Depreciation	Ending Book Value

Plant asset:		Original cost:	
Depreciation method:		Estimated salvage value:	
		Estimated useful life:	

Year	Beginning Book Value	Annual Depreciation	Accumulated Depreciation	Ending Book Value

21-3 APPLICATION PROBLEM, p. 567

Preparing plant asset records

These plant asset records are needed to complete Application Problem 21-5.

PLANT ASSET RECORD No. _____   General Ledger Account No. _1215_

Description _____   General Ledger Account _Store Equipment_

Date   Serial
Bought _____   Number _____   Original Cost _____

                        Estimated
Estimated   Salvage   Depreciation
Useful Life _____   Value _____   Method _____

Disposed of: Discarded _____   Sold _____   Traded _____
Date _____   Disposal Amount _____

Year	Annual Depreciation Expense	Accumulated Depreciation	Ending Book Value

Continue record on back of card

PLANT ASSET RECORD No. _____   General Ledger Account No. __1205__

Description _____   General Ledger Account Office Equipment

Date   Serial
Bought _____   Number _____   Original Cost _____

                    Estimated
Estimated   Salvage   Depreciation
Useful Life _____ Value _____   Method _____

Disposed of: Discarded _____ Sold _____ Traded _____
Date _____   Disposal Amount _____

Year	Annual Depreciation Expense	Accumulated Depreciation	Ending Book Value

Continue record on back of card

21-3 APPLICATION PROBLEM (concluded)

PLANT ASSET RECORD No. _____   General Ledger Account No. <u>1215</u>

Description _____   General Ledger Account <u>Store Equipment</u>

Date   Serial
Bought _____ Number _____ Original Cost _____

Estimated   Estimated
                        Salvage   Depreciation
Useful Life _____ Value _____   Method _____

Disposed of: Discarded _____   Sold _____   Traded _____
Date _____   Disposal Amount _____

Year	Annual Depreciation Expense	Accumulated Depreciation	Ending Book Value

Continue record on back of card

Extra form

PLANT ASSET RECORD No. _____   General Ledger Account No. _____

Description _____   General Ledger Account _____

Date   Serial

Bought _____   Number _____   Original Cost _____

                             Estimated

Estimated   Salvage   Depreciation

Useful Life _____   Value _____   Method _____

Disposed of: Discarded _____   Sold _____   Traded _____

Date _____   Disposal Amount _____

Year	Annual Depreciation Expense	Accumulated Depreciation	Ending Book Value

Continue record on back of card

21-4 **APPLICATION PROBLEM, p. 568**

Journalizing annual depreciation expense

Baumann, Inc.

Work Sheet

For Year Ended December 31, 20 – –

	ACCOUNT TITLE	TRIAL BALANCE		ADJUSTMENTS	
		DEBIT	CREDIT	DEBIT	CREDIT
10	Office Equipment	87 1 5 4 00			
11	Accumulated Depreciation—Office Equipment		31 5 8 0 00		
38	Depreciation Expense—Office Equipment				

GENERAL JOURNAL   PAGE 13

	DATE	ACCOUNT TITLE	DOC. NO.	POST. REF.	DEBIT	CREDIT	
1							1
2							2
3							3
4							4

GENERAL LEDGER

ACCOUNT Office Equipment   ACCOUNT NO. 1205

DATE	ITEM	POST. REF.	DEBIT	CREDIT	BALANCE DEBIT	BALANCE CREDIT
20– – Dec. 31	Balance	✔			87 1 5 4 00	

ACCOUNT Accumulated Depreciation—Office Equipment   ACCOUNT NO. 1210

DATE	ITEM	POST. REF.	DEBIT	CREDIT	BALANCE DEBIT	BALANCE CREDIT
20– – Jan. 1	Balance	✔				31 5 8 0 00

ACCOUNT Depreciation Expense—Office Equipment   ACCOUNT NO. 6120

DATE	ITEM	POST. REF.	DEBIT	CREDIT	BALANCE DEBIT	BALANCE CREDIT

Extra form

GENERAL JOURNAL

PAGE

	DATE	ACCOUNT TITLE	DOC. NO.	POST. REF.	DEBIT	CREDIT	
1							1
2							2
3							3
4							4
5							5
6							6
7							7
8							8
9							9
10							10
11							11
12							12
13							13
14							14
15							15
16							16
17							17
18							18
19							19
20							20
21							21
22							22
23							23
24							24
25							25
26							26
27							27
28							28
29							29
30							30
31							31
32							32
33							33

21-5 APPLICATION PROBLEM, p. 568

Recording the disposal of plant assets

1.

GENERAL JOURNAL   PAGE 3

DATE	ACCOUNT TITLE	DOC. NO.	POST. REF.	DEBIT	CREDIT
					1
					2
					3
					4
					5

2.

CASH RECEIPTS JOURNAL   PAGE 3

DATE	ACCOUNT TITLE	DOC. NO.	POST. REF.	GENERAL DEBIT	GENERAL CREDIT	ACCOUNTS RECEIVABLE CREDIT	SALES CREDIT	SALES TAX PAYABLE DEBIT	SALES TAX PAYABLE CREDIT	SALES DISCOUNT DEBIT	CASH DEBIT
											1
											2
											3
											4
											5
											6
											7
											8
											9
											10
											11
											12

Extra form

CASH RECEIPTS JOURNAL

	DATE	ACCOUNT TITLE	DOC. NO.	POST. REF.	GENERAL DEBIT	GENERAL CREDIT	ACCOUNTS RECEIVABLE CREDIT	SALES CREDIT	SALES TAX PAYABLE DEBIT	SALES TAX PAYABLE CREDIT	SALES DISCOUNT DEBIT	CASH DEBIT	
					1	2	3	4	5	6	7	8	
1													1
2													2
3													3
4													4
5													5
6													6
7													7
8													8
9													9
10													10
11													11
12													12
13													13
14													14
15													15
16													16
17													17
18													18
19													19
20													20
21													21
22													22
23													23
24													24
25													25

21-6 APPLICATION PROBLEM, p. 568

Calculating depreciation using the double declining-balance depreciation method

Plant asset: _____   Original cost: _____
Depreciation method: _____   Estimated salvage value: _____
                                           Estimated useful life: _____

Year	Beginning Book Value	Declining-Balance Rate	Annual Depreciation	Ending Book Value
1				
2				
3				
4				
5				
6				
7				

Plant asset: _____   Original cost: _____
Depreciation method: _____   Estimated salvage value: _____
                                           Estimated useful life: _____

Year	Beginning Book Value	Declining-Balance Rate	Annual Depreciation	Ending Book Value
1				
2				
3				
4				
5				
6				
7				

Plant asset: _____   Original cost: _____
Depreciation method: _____   Estimated salvage value: _____
                                           Estimated useful life: _____

Year	Beginning Book Value	Declining-Balance Rate	Annual Depreciation	Ending Book Value
1				
2				
3				
4				
5				
6				
7				
8				

Extra forms

Plant asset: _____   Original cost: _____
Depreciation method: _____   Estimated salvage value: _____
                                 Estimated useful life: _____

Year	Beginning Book Value	Declining-Balance Rate	Annual Depreciation	Ending Book Value

Plant asset: _____   Original cost: _____
Depreciation method: _____   Estimated salvage value: _____
                                 Estimated useful life: _____

Year	Beginning Book Value	Declining-Balance Rate	Annual Depreciation	Ending Book Value

Plant asset: _____   Original cost: _____
Depreciation method: _____   Estimated salvage value: _____
                                 Estimated useful life: _____

Year	Beginning Book Value	Declining-Balance Rate	Annual Depreciation	Ending Book Value

21-7 MASTERY PROBLEM, p. 568

Recording transactions for plant assets

1.

CASH PAYMENTS JOURNAL

PAGE 1

DATE	ACCOUNT TITLE	CK. NO.	POST. REF.	GENERAL DEBIT	GENERAL CREDIT	ACCOUNTS PAYABLE DEBIT	PURCHASES DISCOUNT CREDIT	CASH CREDIT
				1	2	3	4	5

Extra form

CASH PAYMENTS JOURNAL

PAGE

DATE	ACCOUNT TITLE	CK. NO.	POST. REF.	GENERAL DEBIT	GENERAL CREDIT	ACCOUNTS PAYABLE DEBIT	PURCHASES DISCOUNT CREDIT	CASH CREDIT

21-7 MASTERY PROBLEM (continued)

2., 4., 6.

PLANT ASSET RECORD No. _____   General Ledger Account No. _____

Description _____   General Ledger Account _____

Date   Serial
Bought _____   Number _____   Original Cost _____

                              Estimated
Estimated   Salvage   Depreciation
Useful Life _____   Value _____   Method _____

Disposed of: Discarded _____   Sold _____   Traded _____
Date _____   Disposal Amount _____

Year	Annual Depreciation Expense	Accumulated Depreciation	Ending Book Value

Continue record on back of card

2., 4., 6.

PLANT ASSET RECORD No. _____		General Ledger Account No. _____
Description _____		General Ledger Account _____

Date		Serial			
Bought _____		Number _____		Original Cost _____	

		Estimated			
Estimated		Salvage		Depreciation	
Useful Life _____		Value _____		Method _____	

Disposed of:	Discarded _____	Sold _____	Traded _____
Date _____		Disposal Amount _____	

Year	Annual Depreciation Expense	Accumulated Depreciation	Ending Book Value

Continue record on back of card

21-7   MASTERY PROBLEM (continued)

3.

Plant asset: _____   Original cost: _____
Depreciation method: _____   Estimated salvage value: _____
Estimated useful life: _____

Year	Beginning Book Value	Declining-Balance Rate	Annual Depreciation	Ending Book Value

Plant asset: _____   Original cost: _____
Depreciation method: _____   Estimated salvage value: _____
Estimated useful life: _____

Year	Beginning Book Value	Annual Depreciation	Accumulated Depreciation	Ending Book Value

5.

CASH RECEIPTS JOURNAL

PAGE 2

					1 GENERAL	2	3 ACCOUNTS	4	5 SALES TAX PAYABLE	6	7 SALES	8 CASH
DATE	ACCOUNT TITLE	DOC. NO.	POST. REF.		DEBIT	CREDIT	RECEIVABLE CREDIT	SALES CREDIT	DEBIT	CREDIT	DISCOUNT DEBIT	DEBIT
				1								
				2								
				3								
				4								
				5								
				6								
				7								
				8								
				9								
				10								

GENERAL JOURNAL

PAGE 2

DATE	ACCOUNT TITLE	DOC. NO.	POST. REF.		1 DEBIT	2	3	4 CREDIT	5
				1					
				2					
				3					
				4					
				5					

21-8 CHALLENGE PROBLEM, p. 569

Calculating a partial year's depreciation using the double declining-balance method

Plant asset: _____ Original cost: _____
Depreciation method: _____ Estimated salvage value: _____
Estimated useful life: _____

Year	Beginning Book Value	Declining-Balance Rate	Annual Depreciation	Ending Book Value
1				
2				
3				
4				
5				
6				
7				
8				
9				

Plant asset: _____ Original cost: _____
Depreciation method: _____ Estimated salvage value: _____
Estimated useful life: _____

Year	Beginning Book Value	Declining-Balance Rate	Annual Depreciation	Ending Book Value
1				
2				
3				
4				
5				
6				
7				
8				
9				

Plant asset: _____ Original cost: _____

Depreciation method: _____ Estimated salvage value: _____

Estimated useful life: _____

Year	Beginning Book Value	Declining-Balance Rate	Annual Depreciation	Ending Book Value

Plant asset: _____ Original cost: _____

Depreciation method: _____ Estimated salvage value: _____

Estimated useful life: _____

Year	Beginning Book Value	Declining-Balance Rate	Annual Depreciation	Ending Book Value

22-1 WORK TOGETHER, p. 577

Preparing a stock record

STOCK RECORD

Description Cable Adapter   Stock No. XW142

Reorder 9   Minimum 18   Location Aisle 7

1	2	3	4	5	6	7
INCREASES			DECREASES			BALANCE
DATE	PURCHASE INVOICE NO.	QUANTITY	DATE	SALES INVOICE NO.	QUANTITY	QUANTITY
			Oct. 7	1729	1	18

Extra form

STOCK RECORD

Description _____ Stock No. _____

Reorder _____ Minimum _____ Location _____

1	2	3	4	5	6	7
INCREASES			DECREASES			BALANCE
DATE	PURCHASE INVOICE NO.	QUANTITY	DATE	SALES INVOICE NO.	QUANTITY	QUANTITY

Preparing a stock record

STOCK RECORD

Description Crystal Biscuit Barrel   Stock No. C310

Reorder 20   Minimum 15   Location Aisle 6

1	2	3	4	5	6	7
INCREASES			DECREASES			BALANCE
DATE	PURCHASE INVOICE NO.	QUANTITY	DATE	SALES INVOICE NO.	QUANTITY	QUANTITY
			Nov. 29	6120		13

Extra form

STOCK RECORD

Description _____   Stock No. _____

Reorder _____   Minimum _____   Location _____

1	2	3	4	5	6	7
INCREASES			DECREASES			BALANCE
DATE	PURCHASE INVOICE NO.	QUANTITY	DATE	SALES INVOICE NO.	QUANTITY	QUANTITY

22-2 WORK TOGETHER, p. 582

Determining the cost of inventory using the fifo, lifo, and weighted-average inventory costing methods

FIFO method

Purchase Dates	Units Purchased	Unit Price	Total Cost	FIFO Units on Hand	FIFO Cost
January 1, beginning inventory	14	$30.00	$ 420.00		
March 3, purchases	9	32.00	288.00		
July 13, purchases	10	34.00	340.00		
August 15, purchases	8	36.00	288.00		
October 22, purchases	9	38.00	342.00		
Totals	50		$1,678.00		

LIFO method

Purchase Dates	Units Purchased	Unit Price	Total Cost	LIFO Units on Hand	LIFO Cost
January 1, beginning inventory	14	$30.00	$ 420.00		
March 3, purchases	9	32.00	288.00		
July 13, purchases	10	34.00	340.00		
August 15, purchases	8	36.00	288.00		
October 22, purchases	9	38.00	342.00		
Totals	50		$1,678.00		

Weighted-average method

Purchases			Total Cost
Date	Units	Unit Price	
January 1, beginning inventory	14	$30.00	
March 3, purchases	9	32.00	
July 13, purchases	10	34.00	
August 15, purchases	8	36.00	
October 22, purchases	9	38.00	
Totals	50		

Determining the cost of inventory using the fifo, lifo, and weighted-average inventory costing methods

FIFO method

Purchase Dates	Units Purchased	Unit Price	Total Cost	FIFO Units on Hand	FIFO Cost
January 1, beginning inventory	17	$12.00	$ 204.00		
February 3, purchases	24	13.00	312.00		
April 15, purchases	25	14.00	350.00		
September 4, purchases	22	14.50	319.00		
December 9, purchases	20	15.00	300.00		
Totals	108		$1,485.00		

LIFO method

Purchase Dates	Units Purchased	Unit Price	Total Cost	LIFO Units on Hand	LIFO Cost
January 1, beginning inventory	17	$12.00	$ 204.00		
February 3, purchases	24	13.00	312.00		
April 15, purchases	25	14.00	350.00		
September 4, purchases	22	14.50	319.00		
December 9, purchases	20	15.00	300.00		
Totals	108		$1,485.00		

Weighted-average method

Purchases			Total Cost
Date	Units	Unit Price	
January 1, beginning inventory	17	$12.00	
February 3, purchases	24	13.00	
April 15, purchases	25	14.00	
September 4, purchases	22	14.50	
December 9, purchases	20	15.00	
Totals	108		

22-3 WORK TOGETHER, p. 585

Estimating ending inventory using the gross profit method

4.

STEP 1
Beginning inventory, June 1 . . . . _____
Plus net purchases for June 1 to June 30 . . . . _____
Equals cost of merchandise available for sale . . . . _____
STEP 2
Net sales for June 1 to June 30 . . . . _____
Times previous year's gross profit percentage . . . . _____
Equals estimated gross profit on operations . . . . _____
STEP 3
Net sales for June 1 to June 30 . . . . _____
Less estimated gross profit on operations . . . . _____
Equals estimated cost of merchandise sold . . . . _____
STEP 4
Cost of merchandise available for sale . . . . _____
Less estimated cost of merchandise sold . . . . _____
Equals estimated ending merchandise inventory . . . . _____

5.

Evans Company

Income Statement

For Month Ended June 30, 20 – –

		% OF NET SALES
Operating Revenue:		
Net Sales		
Cost of Merchandise Sold:		
Estimated Beginning Inventory, June 1		
Net Purchases		
Merchandise Available for Sale		
Less Estimated Ending Inventory, June 30		
Cost of Merchandise Sold		
Gross Profit on Operations		
Operating Expenses		
Net Income		

Estimating ending inventory using the gross profit method

6.

STEP 1

Beginning inventory, April 1 . . . . _____

Plus net purchases for April 1 to April 30 . . . . _____

Equals cost of merchandise available for sale . . . . _____

STEP 2

Net sales for April 1 to April 30 . . . . _____

Times previous year's gross profit percentage . . . . _____

Equals estimated gross profit on operations . . . . _____

STEP 3

Net sales for April 1 to April 30 . . . . _____

Less estimated gross profit on operations . . . . _____

Equals estimated cost of merchandise sold . . . . _____

STEP 4

Cost of merchandise available for sale . . . . _____

Less estimated cost of merchandise sold . . . . _____

Equals estimated ending merchandise inventory . . . . _____

7.

Tabora Stores										
Income Statement										
For Month Ended April 30, 20 – –									% OF NET SALES	
Operating Revenue:										
Net Sales										
Cost of Merchandise Sold:										
Estimated Beginning Inventory, April 1										
Net Purchases										
Merchandise Available for Sale										
Less Estimated Ending Inventory, April 30										
Cost of Merchandise Sold										
Gross Profit on Operations										
Operating Expenses										
Net Income										

22-1 APPLICATION PROBLEM, p. 587

Preparing a stock record

STOCK RECORD

Description _Speaker Wire_   Stock No. _BE211_

Reorder _90_   Minimum _150_   Location _Aisle C_

1	2	3	4	5	6	7
INCREASES			DECREASES			BALANCE
DATE	PURCHASE INVOICE NO.	QUANTITY	DATE	SALES INVOICE NO.	QUANTITY	QUANTITY
			Nov. 2	3469	50	159

Extra form

STOCK RECORD

Description _____   Stock No. _____

Reorder _____   Minimum _____   Location _____

1	2	3	4	5	6	7
INCREASES			DECREASES			BALANCE
DATE	PURCHASE INVOICE NO.	QUANTITY	DATE	SALES INVOICE NO.	QUANTITY	QUANTITY

STOCK RECORD

Description _____   Stock No. _____
Reorder _____ Minimum _____ Location _____

1	2	3	4	5	6	7
INCREASES			DECREASES			BALANCE
DATE	PURCHASE INVOICE NO.	QUANTITY	DATE	SALES INVOICE NO.	QUANTITY	QUANTITY

STOCK RECORD

Description _____   Stock No. _____
Reorder _____ Minimum _____ Location _____

1	2	3	4	5	6	7
INCREASES			DECREASES			BALANCE
DATE	PURCHASE INVOICE NO.	QUANTITY	DATE	SALES INVOICE NO.	QUANTITY	QUANTITY

22-2 APPLICATION PROBLEM, p. 587

Determining the cost of inventory using the fifo, lifo, and weighted-average inventory costing methods

FIFO method

Purchase Dates	Units Purchased	Unit Price	Total Cost	FIFO Units on Hand	FIFO Cost
January 1, beginning inventory	90	$1.00	$ 90.00		
March 29, purchases	78	1.10	85.80		
May 6, purchases	80	1.25	100.00		
August 28, purchases	84	1.30	109.20		
November 8, purchases	88	1.40	123.20		
Totals	420		$508.20		

LIFO method

Purchase Dates	Units Purchased	Unit Price	Total Cost	LIFO Units on Hand	LIFO Cost
January 1, beginning inventory	90	$1.00	$ 90.00		
March 29, purchases	78	1.10	85.80		
May 6, purchases	80	1.25	100.00		
August 28, purchases	84	1.30	109.20		
November 8, purchases	88	1.40	123.20		
Totals	420		$508.20		

Weighted-average method

Purchases			Total Cost
Date	Units	Unit Price	
January 1, beginning inventory	90	$1.00	
March 29, purchases	78	1.10	
May 6, purchases	80	1.25	
August 28, purchases	84	1.30	
November 8, purchases	88	1.40	
Totals	420		

Extra forms

FIFO method

Purchase Dates	Units Purchased	Unit Price	Total Cost	FIFO Units on Hand	FIFO Cost

LIFO method

Purchase Dates	Units Purchased	Unit Price	Total Cost	LIFO Units on Hand	LIFO Cost

Weighted-average method

Purchases			Total Cost
Date	Units	Unit Price	

22-3 APPLICATION PROBLEM, p. 587

Estimating ending inventory using the gross profit method

1.

STEP 1

Beginning inventory, August 1 . . . . _____

Plus net purchases for August 1 to August 31 . . . . _____

Equals cost of merchandise available for sale . . . . _____

STEP 2

Net sales for August 1 to August 31 . . . . _____

Times previous year's gross profit percentage . . . . _____

Equals estimated gross profit on operations . . . . _____

STEP 3

Net sales for August 1 to August 31 . . . . _____

Less estimated gross profit on operations . . . . _____

Equals estimated cost of merchandise sold . . . . _____

STEP 4

Cost of merchandise available for sale . . . . _____

Less estimated cost of merchandise sold . . . . _____

Equals estimated ending merchandise inventory . . . . _____

2.

Cutshaw Company

Income Statement

For Month Ended August 31, 20 – –

						% OF NET SALES
Operating Revenue:						
Net Sales						
Cost of Merchandise Sold:						
Estimated Beginning Inventory, August 1						
Net Purchases						
Merchandise Available for Sale						
Less Estimated Ending Inventory, August 31						
Cost of Merchandise Sold						
Gross Profit on Operations						
Operating Expenses						
Net Income						

Extra form

										% OF NET SALES

22-4 MASTERY PROBLEM, p. 588

Determining the cost of inventory using the fifo, lifo, and weighted-average inventory costing methods

1. **FIFO method**

Purchase Dates	Units Purchased	Unit Price	Total Cost	FIFO Units on Hand	FIFO Cost
January 1, beginning inventory					
January 8, purchases					
April 2, purchases					
September 13, purchases					
December 20, purchases					
Totals					

LIFO method

Purchase Dates	Units Purchased	Unit Price	Total Cost	FIFO Units on Hand	FIFO Cost
January 1, beginning inventory					
January 8, purchases					
April 2, purchases					
September 13, purchases					
December 20, purchases					
Totals					

Weighted-average method

Date	Units	Unit Price	Total Cost
January 1, beginning inventory			
January 8, purchases			
April 2, purchases			
September 13, purchases			
December 20, purchases			
Totals			

2.

	Fifo	Lifo	Weighted-Average
Merchandise Available for Sale			
Ending Inventory			
Cost of Merchandise Sold			

Highest Cost of Merchandise Sold: _____

Extra forms

FIFO method

Purchase Dates	Units Purchased	Unit Price	Total Cost	FIFO Units on Hand	FIFO Cost

LIFO method

Purchase Dates	Units Purchased	Unit Price	Total Cost	LIFO Units on Hand	LIFO Cost

Weighted-average method

Purchases			Total Cost
Date	Units	Unit Price	

22-5 CHALLENGE PROBLEM, p. 588

Determining the cost of merchandise inventory destroyed in a fire

1.

Gross profit on operations .... _____

Divided by net sales .... _____

Equals gross profit percentage of net sales (prior year) .... _____

2.

STEP 1

Beginning inventory, August 1 .... _____

Plus net purchases for August 1 to October 10 .... _____

Equals cost of merchandise available for sale .... _____

STEP 2

Net sales for August 1 to October 10 .... _____

Times prior year's gross profit percentage .... _____

Equals estimated gross profit on operations .... _____

STEP 3

Net sales for August 1 to October 10 .... _____

Less estimated gross profit on operations .... _____

Equals estimated cost of merchandise sold .... _____

STEP 4

Cost of merchandise available for sale .... _____

Less estimated cost of merchandise sold .... _____

Equals estimated ending merchandise inventory .... _____

3.

Estimated merchandise inventory, October 10 .... _____

Less cost of merchandise inventory not destroyed .... _____

Equals estimated cost of merchandise inventory destroyed .... _____

4.

Wright Plumbing Company

Income Statement

For the Period August 1 to October 10, 20 – –

			% OF NET SALES
Operating Revenue:			
Net Sales			
Cost of Merchandise Sold:			
Estimated Beginning Inventory, August 1			
Net Purchases			
Merchandise Available for Sale			
Less Estimated Ending Inventory, October 10			
Cost of Merchandise Sold			
Gross Profit on Operations			
Operating Expenses			
Net Income			

23-1 WORK TOGETHER, p. 597

Calculating interest, maturity dates, and maturity values for promissory notes

Date	Principal	Interest Rate	Time	Interest	Maturity Date	Maturity Value
March 3	$6,000.00	12%	90 days			
March 18	$2,000.00	18%	60 days			

Use this space for calculations:

Extra form

Date	Principal	Interest Rate	Time	Interest	Maturity Date	Maturity Value

23-1 ON YOUR OWN, p. 597

Calculating interest, maturity dates, and maturity values for promissory notes

Date	Principal	Interest Rate	Time	Interest	Maturity Date	Maturity Value
June 6	$10,000.00	10%	60 days			
June 23	$4,200.00	18%	90 days			

Use this space for calculations:

Extra form

Date	Principal	Interest Rate	Time	Interest	Maturity Date	Maturity Value

194 • Working Papers

COPYRIGHT © SOUTH-WESTERN EDUCATIONAL PUBLISHING

23-2 **WORK TOGETHER, p. 602**

Journalizing notes payable transactions

3.

GENERAL JOURNAL

PAGE 3

DATE	ACCOUNT TITLE	DOC. NO.	POST. REF.	DEBIT	CREDIT

3.

CASH RECEIPTS JOURNAL

PAGE 5

				1 GENERAL DEBIT	2 GENERAL CREDIT	3 ACCOUNTS RECEIVABLE CREDIT	4 SALES CREDIT	5 SALES TAX PAYABLE DEBIT	6 SALES TAX PAYABLE CREDIT	7 SALES DISCOUNT DEBIT	8 CASH DEBIT
DATE	ACCOUNT TITLE	DOC. NO.	POST. REF.								

4.

CASH PAYMENTS JOURNAL

PAGE 9

				1 GENERAL DEBIT	2 GENERAL CREDIT	3 ACCOUNTS PAYABLE DEBIT	4 PURCHASES DISCOUNT CREDIT	5 CASH CREDIT
DATE	ACCOUNT TITLE	CK. NO.	POST. REF.					

Journalizing notes payable transactions

5.

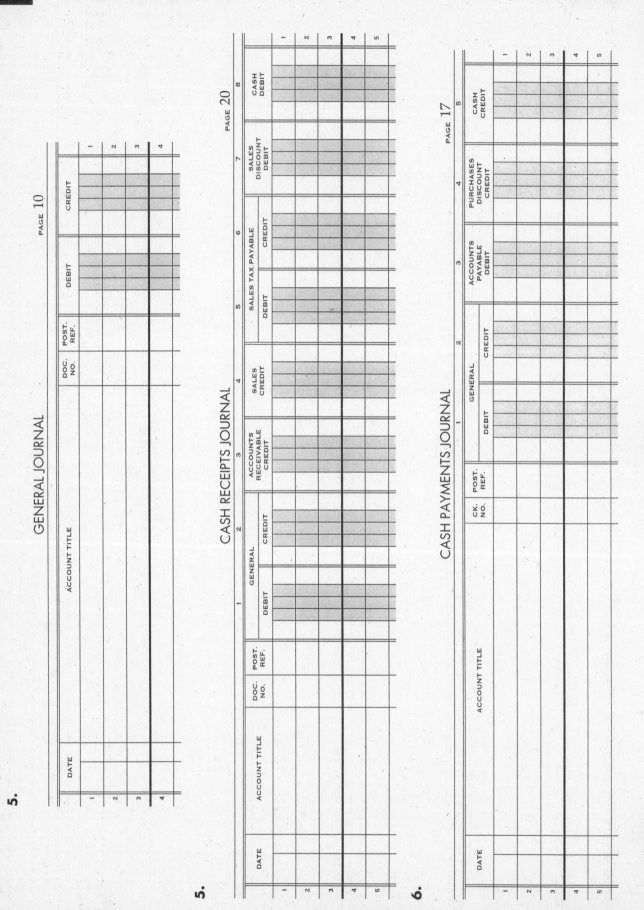

GENERAL JOURNAL

PAGE 10

DATE	ACCOUNT TITLE	DOC. NO.	POST. REF.	DEBIT	CREDIT

CASH RECEIPTS JOURNAL

PAGE 20

				1 GENERAL DEBIT	2 GENERAL CREDIT	3 ACCOUNTS RECEIVABLE CREDIT	4 SALES CREDIT	5 SALES TAX PAYABLE DEBIT	6 SALES TAX PAYABLE CREDIT	7 SALES DISCOUNT DEBIT	8 CASH DEBIT
DATE	ACCOUNT TITLE	DOC. NO.	POST. REF.								

CASH PAYMENTS JOURNAL

PAGE 17

				1 GENERAL DEBIT	2 GENERAL CREDIT	3 ACCOUNTS PAYABLE DEBIT	4 PURCHASES DISCOUNT CREDIT	5 CASH CREDIT
DATE	ACCOUNT TITLE	CK. NO.	POST. REF.					

6.

23-3 WORK TOGETHER, p. 606

Journalizing notes receivable transactions

GENERAL JOURNAL

PAGE 2

DATE	ACCOUNT TITLE	DOC. NO.	POST. REF.	DEBIT	CREDIT	
						1
						2
						3
						4
						5
						6

CASH RECEIPTS JOURNAL

PAGE 3

				1 GENERAL		2 ACCOUNTS RECEIVABLE CREDIT	3 SALES CREDIT	4 SALES TAX PAYABLE		5 SALES DISCOUNT DEBIT	6 CASH DEBIT	
DATE	ACCOUNT TITLE	DOC. NO.	POST. REF.	DEBIT	CREDIT			DEBIT	CREDIT			
												1
												2
												3
												4
												5

Journalizing notes receivable transactions

GENERAL JOURNAL

PAGE 3

DATE	ACCOUNT TITLE	DOC. NO.	POST. REF.	DEBIT	CREDIT	
						1
						2
						3
						4
						5
						6

CASH RECEIPTS JOURNAL

PAGE 5

				1	2	3	4	5	6	7	8
DATE	ACCOUNT TITLE	DOC. NO.	POST. REF.	GENERAL DEBIT	GENERAL CREDIT	ACCOUNTS RECEIVABLE CREDIT	SALES CREDIT	SALES TAX PAYABLE DEBIT	SALES TAX PAYABLE CREDIT	SALES DISCOUNT DEBIT	CASH DEBIT

Name _____ Date _____ Class _____

23-1 APPLICATION PROBLEM, p. 608

Calculating interest, maturity dates, and maturity values for promissory notes

Date	Principal	Interest Rate	Time	Interest	Maturity Date	Maturity Value
April 2	$10,000.00	12%	180 days			
April 8	$600.00	18%	60 days			
April 15	$5,000.00	14%	90 days			
April 18	$1,200.00	18%	60 days			

Use this space for calculations:

Extra form

Date	Principal	Interest Rate	Time	Interest	Maturity Date	Maturity Value

Extra forms

Date	Principal	Interest Rate	Time	Interest	Maturity Date	Maturity Value

Date	Principal	Interest Rate	Time	Interest	Maturity Date	Maturity Value

Date	Principal	Interest Rate	Time	Interest	Maturity Date	Maturity Value

23-2 **APPLICATION PROBLEM, p. 608**

Journalizing notes payable transactions

1.

GENERAL JOURNAL

PAGE 4

DATE	ACCOUNT TITLE	DOC. NO.	POST. REF.	DEBIT	CREDIT

CASH RECEIPTS JOURNAL

PAGE 6

				GENERAL		ACCOUNTS RECEIVABLE CREDIT	SALES CREDIT	SALES TAX PAYABLE		SALES DISCOUNT DEBIT	CASH DEBIT
DATE	ACCOUNT TITLE	DOC. NO.	POST. REF.	DEBIT	CREDIT			DEBIT	CREDIT		

CASH PAYMENTS JOURNAL

PAGE 9

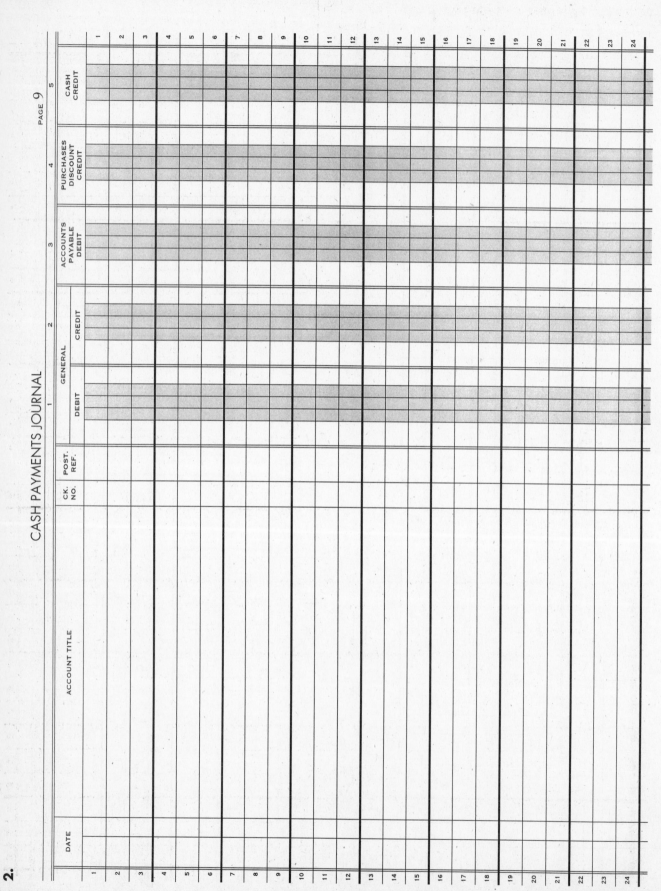

Name _____ Date _____ Class _____

Journalizing notes receivable transactions

GENERAL JOURNAL   PAGE 12

	DATE	ACCOUNT TITLE	DOC. NO.	POST. REF.	DEBIT	CREDIT	
1							1
2							2
3							3
4							4
5							5
6							6
7							7
8							8
9							9
10							10
11							11
12							12
13							13
14							14
15							15
16							16
17							17
18							18
19							19
20							20
21							21
22							22
23							23
24							24
25							25
26							26
27							27
28							28
29							29
30							30
31							31
32							32
33							33

CASH RECEIPTS JOURNAL

PAGE 8

	DATE	ACCOUNT TITLE	DOC. NO.	POST. REF.	GENERAL DEBIT	GENERAL CREDIT	ACCOUNTS RECEIVABLE CREDIT	SALES CREDIT	SALES TAX PAYABLE DEBIT	SALES TAX PAYABLE CREDIT	SALES DISCOUNT DEBIT	CASH DEBIT
1												
2												
3												
4												
5												
6												
7												
8												
9												
10												
11												
12												
13												
14												
15												
16												
17												
18												
19												
20												
21												
22												
23												
24												
25												

23-4 APPLICATION PROBLEM, p. 609

Journalizing notes receivable transactions

GENERAL JOURNAL   PAGE 18

	DATE		ACCOUNT TITLE	DOC. NO.	POST. REF.	DEBIT	CREDIT	
1								1
2								2
3								3
4								4
5								5
6								6
7								7
8								8
9								9
10								10
11								11
12								12
13								13
14								14
15								15
16								16
17								17
18								18
19								19
20								20
21								21
22								22
23								23
24								24
25								25
26								26
27								27
28								28
29								29
30								30
31								31
32								32
33								33

PAGE 11

CASH RECEIPTS JOURNAL

| | | | | GENERAL | | ACCOUNTS RECEIVABLE CREDIT | SALES CREDIT | SALES TAX PAYABLE | | SALES DISCOUNT DEBIT | CASH DEBIT |
DATE	ACCOUNT TITLE	DOC. NO.	POST. REF.	DEBIT	CREDIT			DEBIT	CREDIT		
				1	2	3	4	5	6	7	8

23-5 **MASTERY PROBLEM, p. 610**

Journalizing notes payable and notes receivable transactions

1.

GENERAL JOURNAL

PAGE 3

DATE	ACCOUNT TITLE	DOC. NO.	POST. REF.	DEBIT	CREDIT

CASH RECEIPTS JOURNAL

PAGE 6

DATE	ACCOUNT TITLE	DOC. NO.	POST. REF.	GENERAL DEBIT	GENERAL CREDIT	ACCOUNTS RECEIVABLE CREDIT	SALES CREDIT	SALES TAX PAYABLE DEBIT	SALES TAX PAYABLE CREDIT	SALES DISCOUNT DEBIT	CASH DEBIT

2.

23-5 MASTERY PROBLEM (concluded)

3.

CASH PAYMENTS JOURNAL

PAGE 9

DATE	ACCOUNT TITLE	CK. NO.	POST. REF.	GENERAL DEBIT	GENERAL CREDIT	ACCOUNTS PAYABLE DEBIT	PURCHASES DISCOUNT CREDIT	CASH CREDIT

Extra form

CASH PAYMENTS JOURNAL

PAGE

DATE	ACCOUNT TITLE	CK. NO.	POST. REF.	GENERAL DEBIT	GENERAL CREDIT	ACCOUNTS PAYABLE DEBIT	PURCHASES DISCOUNT CREDIT	CASH CREDIT
				1	2	3	4	5

23-6 CHALLENGE PROBLEM, p. 610

Recording notes receivable stated in months

1.

2.

3.

4.

Extra form

24-1 WORK TOGETHER, p. 620

Journalizing and posting entries for accrued revenue

3.

Wrenn Corporation

Work Sheet

For Year Ended December 31, 20 – –

	ACCOUNT TITLE	TRIAL BALANCE		ADJUSTMENTS	
		DEBIT	CREDIT	DEBIT	CREDIT
4	Interest Receivable				
50	Interest Income		1 5 4 5 00		

4., 5.

GENERAL JOURNAL   PAGE 14

	DATE	ACCOUNT TITLE	DOC. NO.	POST. REF.	DEBIT	CREDIT	
1							1
2							2
3							3
4							4
5							5
6							6
7							7
8							8

6.

GENERAL JOURNAL   PAGE 15

	DATE	ACCOUNT TITLE	DOC. NO.	POST. REF.	DEBIT	CREDIT	
1							1
2							2
3							3
4							4

Journalizing and posting entries for accrued revenue

8.

Sierra, Inc.

Work Sheet

For Year Ended December 31, 20 – –

		1	2	3	4
	ACCOUNT TITLE	TRIAL BALANCE		ADJUSTMENTS	
		DEBIT	CREDIT	DEBIT	CREDIT
4	Interest Receivable				
50	Interest Income		9 8 7 00		

9., 10.

GENERAL JOURNAL   PAGE 14

	DATE	ACCOUNT TITLE	DOC. NO.	POST. REF.	DEBIT	CREDIT	
1							1
2							2
3							3
4							4
5							5
6							6
7							7
8							8

11.

GENERAL JOURNAL   PAGE 15

	DATE	ACCOUNT TITLE	DOC. NO.	POST. REF.	DEBIT	CREDIT	
1							1
2							2
3							3
4							4

24-1 WORK TOGETHER (continued)

7.

CASH RECEIPTS JOURNAL

PAGE 16

| | | | GENERAL | | ACCOUNTS RECEIVABLE CREDIT | SALES CREDIT | SALES TAX PAYABLE | | SALES DISCOUNT DEBIT | CASH DEBIT |
DATE	ACCOUNT TITLE	DOC. NO.	POST. REF.	DEBIT	CREDIT			DEBIT	CREDIT		

CASH RECEIPTS JOURNAL

PAGE 19

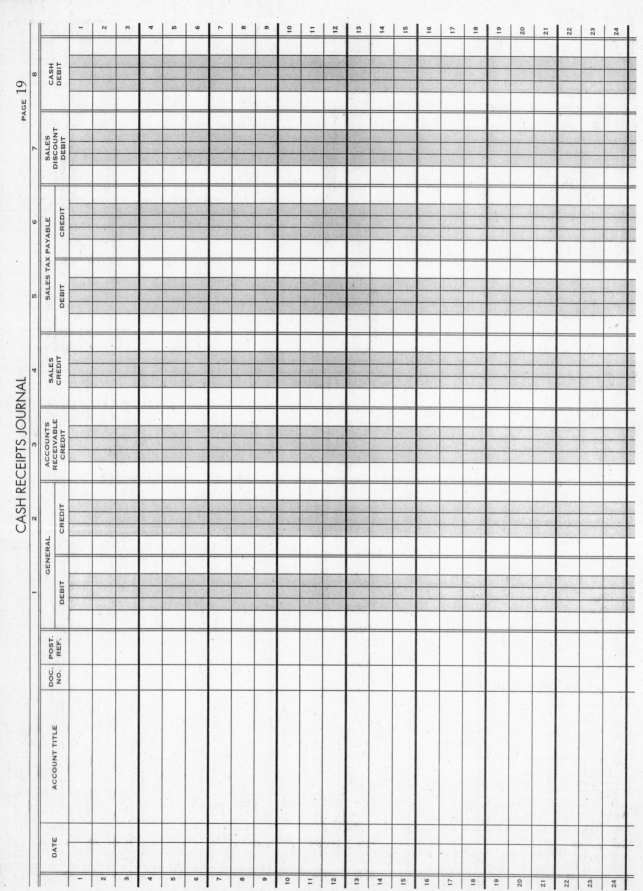

12.

24-1 WORK TOGETHER (concluded)

4., 5., 6., 7.   **GENERAL LEDGER**

ACCOUNT Notes Receivable   ACCOUNT NO. 1115

DATE	ITEM	POST. REF.	DEBIT	CREDIT	BALANCE DEBIT	BALANCE CREDIT
Nov. 16		G11	3 0 0 0 00		3 0 0 0 00	

ACCOUNT Interest Receivable   ACCOUNT NO. 1120

DATE	ITEM	POST. REF.	DEBIT	CREDIT	BALANCE DEBIT	BALANCE CREDIT

ACCOUNT Income Summary   ACCOUNT NO. 3120

DATE	ITEM	POST. REF.	DEBIT	CREDIT	BALANCE DEBIT	BALANCE CREDIT

ACCOUNT Interest Income   ACCOUNT NO. 7110

DATE	ITEM	POST. REF.	DEBIT	CREDIT	BALANCE DEBIT	BALANCE CREDIT
Dec. 31		CR15		1 5 00		1 5 4 5 00

ON YOUR OWN (concluded)

9., 10., 11., 12.   **GENERAL LEDGER**

ACCOUNT Notes Receivable   ACCOUNT NO. 1115

DATE	ITEM	POST. REF.	DEBIT	CREDIT	BALANCE DEBIT	BALANCE CREDIT
Dec. 1		G11	4 0 0 0 00		4 0 0 0 00	

ACCOUNT Interest Receivable   ACCOUNT NO. 1120

DATE	ITEM	POST. REF.	DEBIT	CREDIT	BALANCE DEBIT	BALANCE CREDIT

ACCOUNT Income Summary   ACCOUNT NO. 3120

DATE	ITEM	POST. REF.	DEBIT	CREDIT	BALANCE DEBIT	BALANCE CREDIT

ACCOUNT Interest Income   ACCOUNT NO. 7110

DATE	ITEM	POST. REF.	DEBIT	CREDIT	BALANCE DEBIT	BALANCE CREDIT
Dec. 31		CR15		3 7 50		9 8 7 00

24-2 WORK TOGETHER, p. 626

Journalizing and posting entries for accrued expenses

3.

Powers Corporation

Work Sheet

For Year Ended December 31, 20 – –

		1	2	3	4
	ACCOUNT TITLE	TRIAL BALANCE		ADJUSTMENTS	
		DEBIT	CREDIT	DEBIT	CREDIT
15	Interest Payable				
51	Interest Expense	8 4 6 7 00			

4., 5.

GENERAL JOURNAL   PAGE 14

	DATE	ACCOUNT TITLE	DOC. NO.	POST. REF.	DEBIT	CREDIT	
1							1
2							2
3							3
4							4
5							5
6							6
7							7
8							8

6.

GENERAL JOURNAL   PAGE 15

	DATE	ACCOUNT TITLE	DOC. NO.	POST. REF.	DEBIT	CREDIT	
1							1
2							2
3							3
4							4

Journalizing and posting entries for accrued expenses

8.

Bartlett Industries

Work Sheet

For Year Ended December 31, 20 – –

	ACCOUNT TITLE	TRIAL BALANCE		ADJUSTMENTS	
		1 DEBIT	**2** CREDIT	**3** DEBIT	**4** CREDIT
15	Interest Payable				
51	Interest Expense	10 1 5 7 00			

9., 10.

GENERAL JOURNAL

PAGE 14

	DATE	ACCOUNT TITLE	DOC. NO.	POST. REF.	DEBIT	CREDIT	
1							1
2							2
3							3
4							4
5							5
6							6
7							7
8							8

11.

GENERAL JOURNAL

PAGE 15

	DATE	ACCOUNT TITLE	DOC. NO.	POST. REF.	DEBIT	CREDIT	
1							1
2							2
3							3
4							4

7.

CASH PAYMENTS JOURNAL

PAGE 25

	DATE	ACCOUNT TITLE	CK. NO.	POST. REF.	GENERAL DEBIT (1)	GENERAL CREDIT (2)	ACCOUNTS PAYABLE DEBIT (3)	PURCHASES DISCOUNT CREDIT (4)	CASH CREDIT (5)
1									
2									
3									
4									
5									
6									
7									
8									
9									
10									
11									
12									
13									
14									
15									
16									
17									
18									
19									
20									
21									
22									
23									
24									

12.

CASH PAYMENTS JOURNAL

PAGE 29

				1	2	3	4	5
DATE	ACCOUNT TITLE	CK. NO.	POST. REF.	GENERAL DEBIT	GENERAL CREDIT	ACCOUNTS PAYABLE DEBIT	PURCHASES DISCOUNT CREDIT	CASH CREDIT

24-2 WORK TOGETHER (concluded)

4., 5., 6., 7.   **GENERAL LEDGER**

ACCOUNT **Notes Payable**   ACCOUNT NO. 2105

DATE	ITEM	POST. REF.	DEBIT	CREDIT	BALANCE DEBIT	BALANCE CREDIT
Dec. 1		CR13		2 0 0 0 00		2 0 0 0 00

ACCOUNT **Interest Payable**   ACCOUNT NO. 2110

DATE	ITEM	POST. REF.	DEBIT	CREDIT	BALANCE DEBIT	BALANCE CREDIT

ACCOUNT **Income Summary**   ACCOUNT NO. 3120

DATE	ITEM	POST. REF.	DEBIT	CREDIT	BALANCE DEBIT	BALANCE CREDIT

ACCOUNT **Interest Expense**   ACCOUNT NO. 8105

DATE	ITEM	POST. REF.	DEBIT	CREDIT	BALANCE DEBIT	BALANCE CREDIT
Dec. 31		CP19	1 6 0 00		8 4 6 7 00	

ON YOUR OWN (concluded)

9., 10., 11., 12.   **GENERAL LEDGER**

ACCOUNT Notes Payable   ACCOUNT NO. 2105

DATE	ITEM	POST. REF.	DEBIT	CREDIT	BALANCE DEBIT	BALANCE CREDIT
Sept. 2		CR9		10 000 00		10 000 00

ACCOUNT Interest Payable   ACCOUNT NO. 2110

DATE	ITEM	POST. REF.	DEBIT	CREDIT	BALANCE DEBIT	BALANCE CREDIT

ACCOUNT Income Summary   ACCOUNT NO. 3120

DATE	ITEM	POST. REF.	DEBIT	CREDIT	BALANCE DEBIT	BALANCE CREDIT

ACCOUNT Interest Expense   ACCOUNT NO. 8105

DATE	ITEM	POST. REF.	DEBIT	CREDIT	BALANCE DEBIT	BALANCE CREDIT
Dec. 31		CP21	1 60 00		10 157 00	

24-1 APPLICATION PROBLEM, p. 628

Journalizing and posting entries for accrued revenue

1.

Harris Lumber Company

Work Sheet

For Year Ended December 31, 20 – –

		1	2	3	4
	ACCOUNT TITLE	TRIAL BALANCE		ADJUSTMENTS	
		DEBIT	CREDIT	DEBIT	CREDIT
4	Interest Receivable				
50	Interest Income		2 8 4 3 00		

2., 3.

GENERAL JOURNAL   PAGE 14

	DATE	ACCOUNT TITLE	DOC. NO.	POST. REF.	DEBIT	CREDIT	
1							1
2							2
3							3
4							4
5							5
6							6
7							7
8							8

4.

GENERAL JOURNAL   PAGE 15

	DATE	ACCOUNT TITLE	DOC. NO.	POST. REF.	DEBIT	CREDIT	
1							1
2							2
3							3
4							4

5.

CASH RECEIPTS JOURNAL

PAGE 19

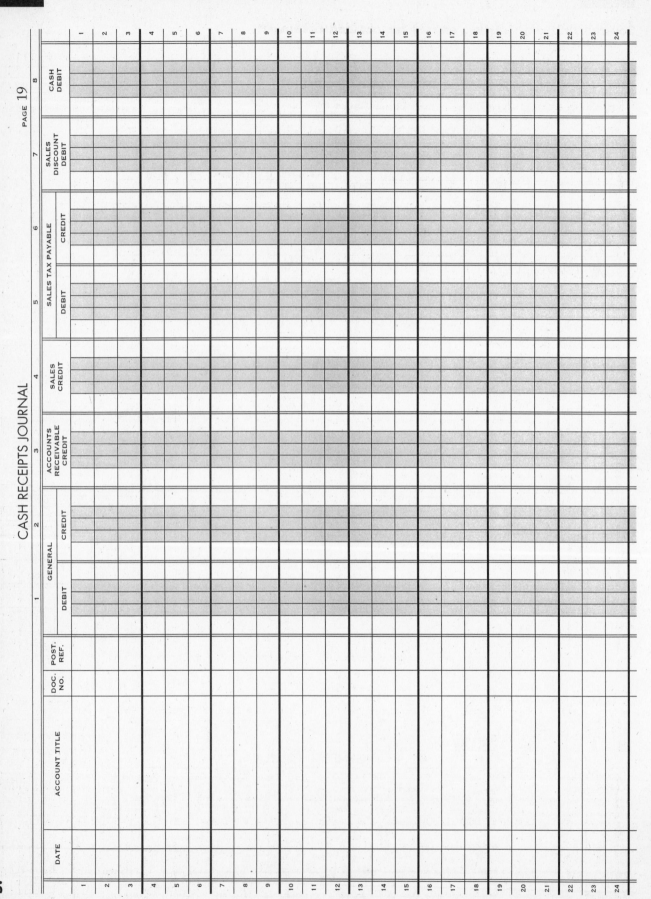

DATE	ACCOUNT TITLE	DOC. NO.	POST. REF.	GENERAL DEBIT	GENERAL CREDIT	ACCOUNTS RECEIVABLE CREDIT	SALES CREDIT	SALES TAX PAYABLE DEBIT	SALES TAX PAYABLE CREDIT	SALES DISCOUNT DEBIT	CASH DEBIT

24-1 APPLICATION PROBLEM (concluded)

2., 3., 4., 5.   **GENERAL LEDGER**

ACCOUNT Notes Receivable   ACCOUNT NO. 1115

DATE	ITEM	POST. REF.	DEBIT	CREDIT	BALANCE DEBIT	BALANCE CREDIT
Nov. 1		G11	2 5 0 0 00		2 5 0 0 00	

ACCOUNT Interest Receivable   ACCOUNT NO. 1120

DATE	ITEM	POST. REF.	DEBIT	CREDIT	BALANCE DEBIT	BALANCE CREDIT

ACCOUNT Income Summary   ACCOUNT NO. 3120

DATE	ITEM	POST. REF.	DEBIT	CREDIT	BALANCE DEBIT	BALANCE CREDIT

ACCOUNT Interest Income   ACCOUNT NO. 7110

DATE	ITEM	POST. REF.	DEBIT	CREDIT	BALANCE DEBIT	BALANCE CREDIT
Dec. 31		CR18		2 5 00		2 8 4 3 00

Extra forms

ACCOUNT _____   ACCOUNT NO. _____

DATE		ITEM	POST. REF.	DEBIT	CREDIT	BALANCE	
						DEBIT	CREDIT

ACCOUNT _____   ACCOUNT NO. _____

DATE		ITEM	POST. REF.	DEBIT	CREDIT	BALANCE	
						DEBIT	CREDIT

ACCOUNT _____   ACCOUNT NO. _____

DATE		ITEM	POST. REF.	DEBIT	CREDIT	BALANCE	
						DEBIT	CREDIT

ACCOUNT _____   ACCOUNT NO. _____

DATE		ITEM	POST. REF.	DEBIT	CREDIT	BALANCE	
						DEBIT	CREDIT

24-2 APPLICATION PROBLEM, p. 628

Journalizing and posting entries for accrued expenses

1.

Delmar Plumbing Supply

Work Sheet

For Year Ended December 31, 20 – –

		ACCOUNT TITLE	TRIAL BALANCE		ADJUSTMENTS	
			1 DEBIT	2 CREDIT	3 DEBIT	4 CREDIT
15		Interest Payable				
51		Interest Expense	8 4 8 9 00			

2., 3.

GENERAL JOURNAL   PAGE 14

	DATE	ACCOUNT TITLE	DOC. NO.	POST. REF.	DEBIT	CREDIT	
1							1
2							2
3							3
4							4
5							5
6							6
7							7
8							8

4.

GENERAL JOURNAL   PAGE 15

	DATE	ACCOUNT TITLE	DOC. NO.	POST. REF.	DEBIT	CREDIT	
1							1
2							2
3							3
4							4

5.

CASH PAYMENTS JOURNAL

PAGE 27

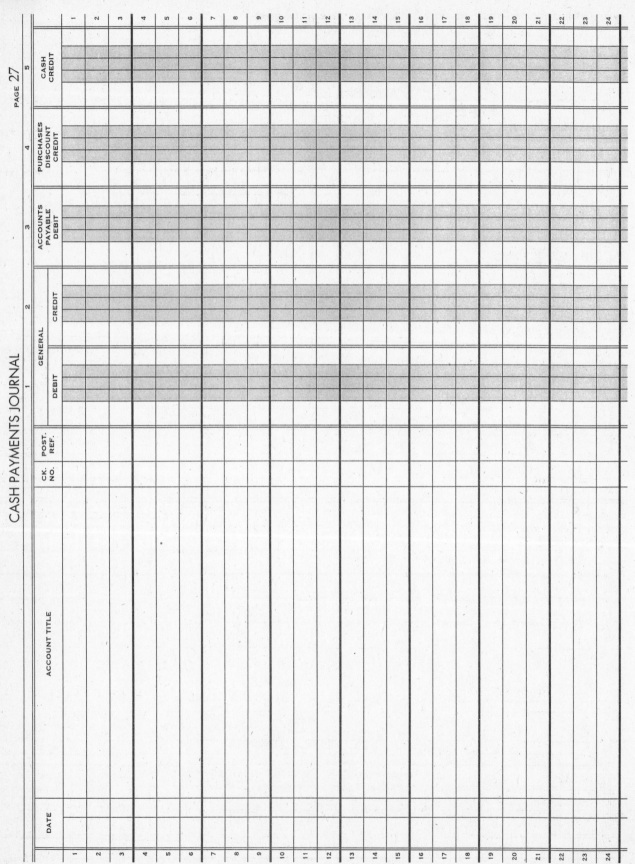

				1 GENERAL DEBIT	2 GENERAL CREDIT	3 ACCOUNTS PAYABLE DEBIT	4 PURCHASES DISCOUNT CREDIT	5 CASH CREDIT	
DATE	ACCOUNT TITLE	CK. NO.	POST. REF.						

Name _____ Date _____ Class _____

24-2 APPLICATION PROBLEM (concluded)

2., 3., 4., 5.   **GENERAL LEDGER**

ACCOUNT Notes Payable   ACCOUNT NO. 2105

DATE	ITEM	POST. REF.	DEBIT	CREDIT	BALANCE DEBIT	BALANCE CREDIT
Dec. 1		CR12		12000 00		12000 00

ACCOUNT Interest Payable   ACCOUNT NO. 2110

DATE	ITEM	POST. REF.	DEBIT	CREDIT	BALANCE DEBIT	BALANCE CREDIT

ACCOUNT Income Summary   ACCOUNT NO. 3120

DATE	ITEM	POST. REF.	DEBIT	CREDIT	BALANCE DEBIT	BALANCE CREDIT

ACCOUNT Interest Expense   ACCOUNT NO. 8105

DATE	ITEM	POST. REF.	DEBIT	CREDIT	BALANCE DEBIT	BALANCE CREDIT
Dec. 31		CP21	160 00		8489 00	

Extra forms

ACCOUNT _____ ACCOUNT NO. _____

DATE		ITEM	POST. REF.	DEBIT	CREDIT	BALANCE	
						DEBIT	CREDIT

ACCOUNT _____ ACCOUNT NO. _____

DATE		ITEM	POST. REF.	DEBIT	CREDIT	BALANCE	
						DEBIT	CREDIT

ACCOUNT _____ ACCOUNT NO. _____

DATE		ITEM	POST. REF.	DEBIT	CREDIT	BALANCE	
						DEBIT	CREDIT

ACCOUNT _____ ACCOUNT NO. _____

DATE		ITEM	POST. REF.	DEBIT	CREDIT	BALANCE	
						DEBIT	CREDIT

24-3 APPLICATION PROBLEM, p. 628

Journalizing and posting entries for accrued expenses

1.

Patti's Dress Shop

Work Sheet

For Year Ended December 31, 20 – –

	ACCOUNT TITLE	TRIAL BALANCE		ADJUSTMENTS	
		DEBIT	CREDIT	DEBIT	CREDIT
15	Interest Payable				
51	Interest Expense	2 8 9 9 00			

2.

GENERAL JOURNAL   PAGE 16

	DATE	ACCOUNT TITLE	DOC. NO.	POST. REF.	DEBIT	CREDIT	
1							1
2							2
3							3
4							4
5							5
6							6
7							7
8							8

GENERAL JOURNAL   PAGE 17

	DATE	ACCOUNT TITLE	DOC. NO.	POST. REF.	DEBIT	CREDIT	
1							1
2							2
3							3
4							4

CASH PAYMENTS JOURNAL

PAGE 23

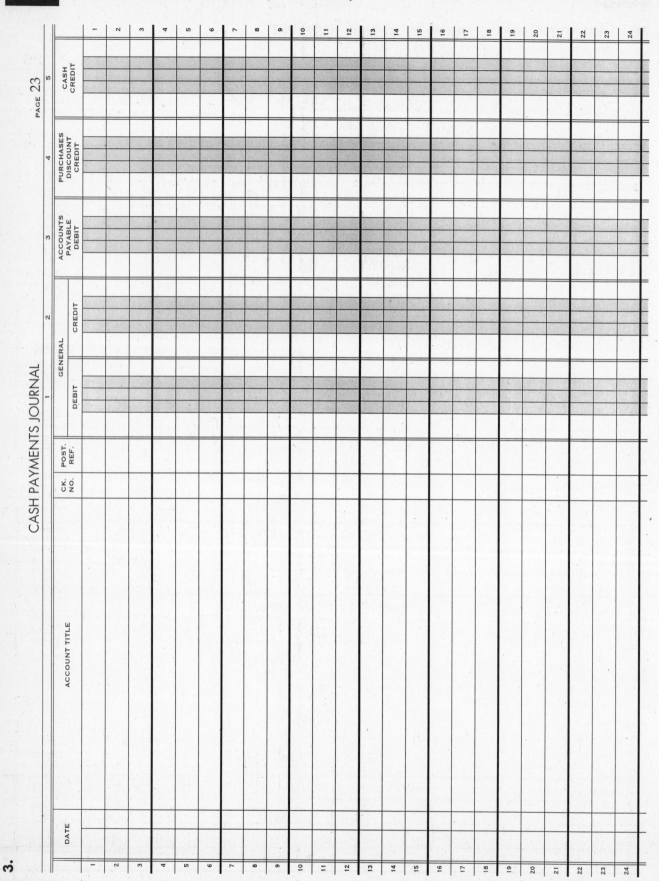

DATE	ACCOUNT TITLE	CK. NO.	POST. REF.	GENERAL DEBIT	GENERAL CREDIT	ACCOUNTS PAYABLE DEBIT	PURCHASES DISCOUNT CREDIT	CASH CREDIT
1								
2								
3								
4								
5								
6								
7								
8								
9								
10								
11								
12								
13								
14								
15								
16								
17								
18								
19								
20								
21								
22								
23								
24								

24-3 APPLICATION PROBLEM (concluded)

2., 3.   GENERAL LEDGER

ACCOUNT Notes Payable   ACCOUNT NO. 2105

DATE	ITEM	POST. REF.	DEBIT	CREDIT	BALANCE DEBIT	BALANCE CREDIT
Oct. 14		CR11		10 0 0 0 00		10 0 0 0 00

ACCOUNT Interest Payable   ACCOUNT NO. 2110

DATE	ITEM	POST. REF.	DEBIT	CREDIT	BALANCE DEBIT	BALANCE CREDIT

ACCOUNT Income Summary   ACCOUNT NO. 3120

DATE	ITEM	POST. REF.	DEBIT	CREDIT	BALANCE DEBIT	BALANCE CREDIT

ACCOUNT Interest Expense   ACCOUNT NO. 8105

DATE	ITEM	POST. REF.	DEBIT	CREDIT	BALANCE DEBIT	BALANCE CREDIT
Dec. 31		CP19	8 0 00		2 8 9 9 00	

Extra forms

ACCOUNT _____ ACCOUNT NO. _____

DATE		ITEM	POST. REF.	DEBIT	CREDIT	BALANCE	
						DEBIT	CREDIT

ACCOUNT _____ ACCOUNT NO. _____

DATE		ITEM	POST. REF.	DEBIT	CREDIT	BALANCE	
						DEBIT	CREDIT

ACCOUNT _____ ACCOUNT NO. _____

DATE		ITEM	POST. REF.	DEBIT	CREDIT	BALANCE	
						DEBIT	CREDIT

ACCOUNT _____ ACCOUNT NO. _____

DATE		ITEM	POST. REF.	DEBIT	CREDIT	BALANCE	
						DEBIT	CREDIT

24-4 MASTERY PROBLEM, p. 629

Journalizing and posting entries for accrued interest revenue and expense

1.

Farris Company

Work Sheet

For Year Ended December 31, 20X1

| | | TRIAL BALANCE | | ADJUSTMENTS | |
	ACCOUNT TITLE	DEBIT	CREDIT	DEBIT	CREDIT
4	Interest Receivable				
15	Interest Payable				
50	Interest Income		1 8 9 7 00		
51	Interest Expense	1 5 4 8 00			

2., 3.

GENERAL JOURNAL   PAGE 15

	DATE	ACCOUNT TITLE	DOC. NO.	POST. REF.	DEBIT	CREDIT	
1							1
2							2
3							3
4							4
5							5
6							6
7							7
8							8
9							9
10							10
11							11

4.

GENERAL JOURNAL   PAGE 16

	DATE	ACCOUNT TITLE	DOC. NO.	POST. REF.	DEBIT	CREDIT	
1							1
2							2
3							3
4							4
5							5

5.

CASH RECEIPTS JOURNAL

PAGE 13

				1	2	3	4	5	6	7	8
				GENERAL		ACCOUNTS RECEIVABLE CREDIT	SALES CREDIT	SALES TAX PAYABLE		SALES DISCOUNT DEBIT	CASH DEBIT
DATE	ACCOUNT TITLE	DOC. NO.	POST. REF.	DEBIT	CREDIT			DEBIT	CREDIT		

6.

CASH PAYMENTS JOURNAL

PAGE 25

				1	2	3	4	5
				GENERAL		ACCOUNTS PAYABLE DEBIT	PURCHASES DISCOUNT CREDIT	CASH CREDIT
DATE	ACCOUNT TITLE	CK. NO.	POST. REF.	DEBIT	CREDIT			

24-4 MASTERY PROBLEM (continued)

2., 3., 4., 5., 6.   **GENERAL LEDGER**

ACCOUNT Notes Receivable   ACCOUNT NO. 1115

DATE		ITEM	POST. REF.	DEBIT	CREDIT	BALANCE DEBIT	BALANCE CREDIT
Nov.	1		G12	6 0 0 00		6 0 0 00	

ACCOUNT Interest Receivable   ACCOUNT NO. 1120

DATE		ITEM	POST. REF.	DEBIT	CREDIT	BALANCE DEBIT	BALANCE CREDIT

ACCOUNT Notes Payable   ACCOUNT NO. 2105

DATE		ITEM	POST. REF.	DEBIT	CREDIT	BALANCE DEBIT	BALANCE CREDIT
Dec.	1		CR12		2 4 0 0 00		2 4 0 0 00

ACCOUNT Interest Payable   ACCOUNT NO. 2110

DATE		ITEM	POST. REF.	DEBIT	CREDIT	BALANCE DEBIT	BALANCE CREDIT

2., 3., 4., 5., 6.   **GENERAL LEDGER**

ACCOUNT Income Summary   ACCOUNT NO. 3120

DATE	ITEM	POST. REF.	DEBIT	CREDIT	BALANCE DEBIT	BALANCE CREDIT

ACCOUNT Interest Income   ACCOUNT NO. 7110

DATE	ITEM	POST. REF.	DEBIT	CREDIT	BALANCE DEBIT	BALANCE CREDIT
Dec. 31		CR12		2 7 50		1 8 9 7 00

ACCOUNT Interest Expense   ACCOUNT NO. 8105

DATE	ITEM	POST. REF.	DEBIT	CREDIT	BALANCE DEBIT	BALANCE CREDIT
Dec. 31		CP19	4 8 50		1 5 4 8 00	

ACCOUNT   ACCOUNT NO.

DATE	ITEM	POST. REF.	DEBIT	CREDIT	BALANCE DEBIT	BALANCE CREDIT

Name _____ Date _____ Class _____

24-5 CHALLENGE PROBLEM, p. 630

Journalizing and posting entries for accrued interest revenue and expenses

1.

Blackwell Corporation

Work Sheet

For Year Ended December 31, 20X1

	ACCOUNT TITLE	TRIAL BALANCE		ADJUSTMENTS	
		DEBIT	CREDIT	DEBIT	CREDIT
4	Interest Receivable				
15	Interest Payable				
50	Interest Income		1 8 9 7 00		
51	Interest Expense	1 6 4 8 00			

2.

GENERAL JOURNAL   PAGE 16

	DATE	ACCOUNT TITLE	DOC. NO.	POST. REF.	DEBIT	CREDIT	
1							1
2							2
3							3
4							4
5							5
6							6
7							7
8							8
9							9
10							10
11							11

GENERAL JOURNAL   PAGE 17

	DATE	ACCOUNT TITLE	DOC. NO.	POST. REF.	DEBIT	CREDIT	
1							1
2							2
3							3
4							4
5							5

3.

GENERAL JOURNAL

PAGE 18

DATE	ACCOUNT TITLE	DOC. NO.	POST. REF.	DEBIT	CREDIT	
						1
						2
						3
						4
						5

CASH PAYMENTS JOURNAL

PAGE 15

DATE	ACCOUNT TITLE	CK. NO.	POST. REF.	GENERAL DEBIT	GENERAL CREDIT	ACCOUNTS PAYABLE DEBIT	PURCHASES DISCOUNT CREDIT	CASH CREDIT	
									1
									2
									3
									4
									5
									6
									7
									8
									9
									10
									11
									12

24-5 CHALLENGE PROBLEM (continued)

2., 3.   **GENERAL LEDGER**

ACCOUNT Notes Receivable   ACCOUNT NO. 1115

DATE	ITEM	POST. REF.	DEBIT	CREDIT	BALANCE DEBIT	BALANCE CREDIT
Dec. 8		G14	9 0 0 00		9 0 0 00	

ACCOUNT Interest Receivable   ACCOUNT NO. 1120

DATE	ITEM	POST. REF.	DEBIT	CREDIT	BALANCE DEBIT	BALANCE CREDIT

ACCOUNT Notes Payable   ACCOUNT NO. 2105

DATE	ITEM	POST. REF.	DEBIT	CREDIT	BALANCE DEBIT	BALANCE CREDIT
Dec. 15		CR12		10 0 0 0 00		10 0 0 0 00

ACCOUNT Interest Payable   ACCOUNT NO. 2110

DATE	ITEM	POST. REF.	DEBIT	CREDIT	BALANCE DEBIT	BALANCE CREDIT

2., 3.   **GENERAL LEDGER**

ACCOUNT Income Summary   ACCOUNT NO. 3120

DATE	ITEM	POST. REF.	DEBIT	CREDIT	BALANCE DEBIT	BALANCE CREDIT

ACCOUNT Interest Income   ACCOUNT NO. 7110

DATE	ITEM	POST. REF.	DEBIT	CREDIT	BALANCE DEBIT	BALANCE CREDIT
Dec. 31		CR12		85 00		1 897 00

ACCOUNT Interest Expense   ACCOUNT NO. 8105

DATE	ITEM	POST. REF.	DEBIT	CREDIT	BALANCE DEBIT	BALANCE CREDIT
Dec. 31		CP12	100 00		1 648 00	

ACCOUNT   ACCOUNT NO.

DATE	ITEM	POST. REF.	DEBIT	CREDIT	BALANCE DEBIT	BALANCE CREDIT

25-1 **WORK TOGETHER, p. 639**

Journalizing dividends

5.

GENERAL JOURNAL

PAGE 12

DATE	ACCOUNT TITLE	DOC. NO.	POST. REF.	DEBIT	CREDIT

6.

CASH PAYMENTS JOURNAL

PAGE 15

DATE	ACCOUNT TITLE	CK. NO.	POST. REF.	GENERAL DEBIT	GENERAL CREDIT	ACCOUNTS PAYABLE DEBIT	PURCHASES DISCOUNT CREDIT	CASH CREDIT

Journalizing dividends

7.

GENERAL JOURNAL

PAGE 24

DATE	ACCOUNT TITLE	DOC. NO.	POST. REF.	DEBIT	CREDIT

8.

CASH PAYMENTS JOURNAL

PAGE 18

				1	2	3	4	5
DATE	ACCOUNT TITLE	CK. NO.	POST. REF.	GENERAL DEBIT	GENERAL CREDIT	ACCOUNTS PAYABLE DEBIT	PURCHASES DISCOUNT CREDIT	CASH CREDIT

Extra form

ACCOUNT TITLE	TRIAL BALANCE		ADJUSTMENTS		INCOME STATEMENT		BALANCE SHEET	
	DEBIT	CREDIT	DEBIT	CREDIT	DEBIT	CREDIT	DEBIT	CREDIT
	1	2	3	4	5	6	7	8

25-2 and 25-3 WORK TOGETHER, pp. 645, 652

25-2 Preparing a work sheet for a corporation
25-3 Completing a work sheet for a corporation

Webster Corporation
Work Sheet
For Year Ended December 31, 20 – –

	ACCOUNT TITLE	TRIAL BALANCE DEBIT	TRIAL BALANCE CREDIT	ADJUSTMENTS DEBIT	ADJUSTMENTS CREDIT	INCOME STATEMENT DEBIT	INCOME STATEMENT CREDIT	BALANCE SHEET DEBIT	BALANCE SHEET CREDIT
1	Cash	95 0 5 2 23							
2	Petty Cash	3 0 0 00							
3	Notes Receivable	10 9 5 2 00							
4	Interest Receivable								
5	Accounts Receivable	70 0 9 4 10							
6	Allowance for Uncoll. Accts.		4 4 64						
7	Merchandise Inventory	64 3 1 6 30							
8	Supplies	2 5 5 2 08							
9	Prepaid Insurance	9 0 7 1 60							
10	Office Equipment	26 9 4 0 00							
11	Accum. Depr.—Office Equip.		6 7 3 5 00						
12	Store Equipment	21 1 9 9 20							
13	Accum. Depr.—Store Equip.		6 3 5 7 40						
14	Notes Payable		14 4 0 0 00						
15	Interest Payable								
16	Accounts Payable		62 0 1 6 18						
17	Employee Income Tax Pay.		1 6 5 2 40						
18	Federal Income Tax Payable								
19	Social Security Tax Payable		1 5 4 9 19						
20	Medicare Tax Payable		3 5 7 51						
21	Sales Tax Payable		6 6 5 2 60						
22	Unemploy. Tax Pay.—Fed.		3 3 44						
23	Unemploy. Tax Pay.—State		2 2 5 72						
24	Health Ins. Premiums Pay.		7 0 2 60						
25	Dividends Payable		10 8 0 0 00						
26	Capital Stock		100 0 0 0 00						
27	Retained Earnings		59 2 4 1 54						
28	Dividends	43 2 0 0 00							

25-2 and 25-3 **WORK TOGETHER (concluded)**

Webster Corporation

Work Sheet (continued)

For Year Ended December 31, 20 – –

| | TRIAL BALANCE | | ADJUSTMENTS | | INCOME STATEMENT | | BALANCE SHEET | |
ACCOUNT TITLE	DEBIT	CREDIT	DEBIT	CREDIT	DEBIT	CREDIT	DEBIT	CREDIT	
29 Income Summary									29
30 Sales		1078 888 30							30
31 Sales Discount	2 002 80								31
32 Sales Ret. and Allowances	8 347 20								32
33 Purchases	737 482 80								33
34 Purchases Discount		5 463 60							34
35 Purchases Ret. and Allow.		2 716 14							35
36 Advertising Expense	15 948 00								36
37 Cash Short and Over	8 15								37
38 Credit Card Fee Expense	11 066 94								38
39 Depr. Exp.—Office Equip.									39
40 Depr. Exp.—Store Equip.									40
41 Insurance Expense									41
42 Miscellaneous Expense	9 682 20								42
43 Payroll Taxes Expense	14 966 00								43
44 Rent Expense	28 915 00								44
45 Repair Expense	3 485 00								45
46 Salary Expense	158 964 00								46
47 Supplies Expense									47
48 Uncollectible Accounts Exp.									48
49 Utilities Expense	2 661 00								49
50 Gain on Plant Assets		1 100 00							50
51 Interest Income		8 914 48							51
52 Interest Expense	2 086 14								52
53 Loss on Plant Assets	2 48 00								53
54 Federal Income Tax Expense	19 300 00								54
55	1358 840 74	1358 840 74							55
56 Net Inc. after Fed. Inc. Tax									56
57									57

4. Total of Income Statement Credit column _____

Less total of Income Statement Debit column before federal income tax _____

Equals Net Income before Federal Income Tax _____

Chapter 25 Distributing Dividends and Preparing a Work Sheet • 249

25-2 and 25-3 ON YOUR OWN, pp. 645, 652

25-2 Preparing a work sheet for a corporation
25-3 Completing a work sheet for a corporation

Osborn Corporation
Work Sheet
For Year Ended December 31, 20 - -

	ACCOUNT TITLE	TRIAL BALANCE DEBIT	TRIAL BALANCE CREDIT	ADJUSTMENTS DEBIT	ADJUSTMENTS CREDIT	INCOME STATEMENT DEBIT	INCOME STATEMENT CREDIT	BALANCE SHEET DEBIT	BALANCE SHEET CREDIT
1	Cash	5 8 4 8 00							
2	Petty Cash	2 5 0 00							
3	Notes Receivable	11 9 5 4 00							
4	Interest Receivable								
5	Accounts Receivable	75 1 7 1 69							
6	Allowance for Uncoll. Accts.		8 0 53						
7	Merchandise Inventory	89 5 4 8 50							
8	Supplies	4 8 3 5 80							
9	Prepaid Insurance	12 5 1 8 00							
10	Office Equipment	35 1 8 4 00							
11	Accum. Depr.—Office Equip.		8 4 7 8 00						
12	Store Equipment	32 1 8 4 50							
13	Accum. Depr.—Store Equip.		12 8 4 8 50						
14	Notes Payable		20 0 0 0 00						
15	Interest Payable								
16	Accounts Payable		24 8 1 8 80						
17	Employee Income Tax Pay.		1 5 8 4 50						
18	Federal Income Tax Payable								
19	Social Security Tax Payable		1 4 8 7 20						
20	Medicare Tax Payable		3 4 3 20						
21	Sales Tax Payable		5 8 4 8 20						
22	Unemploy. Tax Pay.—Fed.		3 0 87						
23	Unemploy. Tax Pay.—State		2 0 5 80						
24	Health Ins. Premiums Pay.		7 0 2 60						
25	Dividends Payable		15 0 0 0 00						
26	Capital Stock		80 0 0 0 00						
27	Retained Earnings		56 1 0 6 89						
28	Dividends	25 0 0 0 00							

25-2 and 25-3 ON YOUR OWN (concluded)

Osborn Corporation
Work Sheet (continued)
For Year Ended December 31, 20 - -

	ACCOUNT TITLE	TRIAL BALANCE DEBIT	TRIAL BALANCE CREDIT	ADJUSTMENTS DEBIT	ADJUSTMENTS CREDIT	INCOME STATEMENT DEBIT	INCOME STATEMENT CREDIT	BALANCE SHEET DEBIT	BALANCE SHEET CREDIT
29	Income Summary								
30	Sales		1184 8 3 5 00						
31	Sales Discount	2 3 1 8 8 80							
32	Sales Ret. and Allowances	9 1 0 5 50							
33	Purchases	858 7 8 9 20							
34	Purchases Discount		6 1 5 4 80						
35	Purchases Ret. and Allow.		3 2 1 8 80						
36	Advertising Expense	1 6 8 4 8 20							
37	Cash Short and Over	1 2 50							
38	Credit Card Fee Expense	1 2 4 8 6 90							
39	Depr. Exp.—Office Equip.								
40	Depr. Exp.—Store Equip.								
41	Insurance Expense								
42	Miscellaneous Expense	1 0 7 8 9 00							
43	Payroll Taxes Expense	1 5 4 8 3 00							
44	Rent Expense	1 9 7 0 0 00							
45	Repair Expense	4 8 4 8 80							
46	Salary Expense	160 3 1 8 50							
47	Supplies Expense								
48	Uncollectible Accounts Exp.								
49	Utilities Expense	8 1 5 3 80							
50	Gain on Plant Assets		5 1 4 00						
51	Interest Income		1 5 8 00						
52	Interest Expense	2 7 3 9 00							
53	Loss on Plant Assets	3 2 8 00							
54	Federal Income Tax Expense	8 0 0 0 00							
55		1422 4 1 5 69	1422 4 1 5 69						
56	Net Inc. after Fed. Inc. Tax								
57									

7. Total of Income Statement Credit column _____

Less total of Income Statement Debit column
    before federal income tax _____

Equals Net Income before Federal Income Tax

Extra form

		ACCOUNT TITLE		TRIAL BALANCE		ADJUSTMENTS		INCOME STATEMENT		BALANCE SHEET	
				DEBIT 1	CREDIT 2	DEBIT 3	CREDIT 4	DEBIT 5	CREDIT 6	DEBIT 7	CREDIT 8
29											
30											
31											
32											
33											
34											
35											
36											
37											
38											
39											
40											
41											
42											
43											
44											
45											
46											
47											
48											
49											
50											
51											
52											
53											
54											
55											
56											
57											

25-1 APPLICATION PROBLEM, p. 654

Journalizing dividends

1.

GENERAL JOURNAL

PAGE 18

DATE	ACCOUNT TITLE	DOC. NO.	POST. REF.	DEBIT	CREDIT

2.

CASH PAYMENTS JOURNAL

PAGE 24

				1 GENERAL	2	3 ACCOUNTS PAYABLE DEBIT	4 PURCHASES DISCOUNT CREDIT	5 CASH CREDIT
DATE	ACCOUNT TITLE	CK. NO.	POST. REF.	DEBIT	CREDIT			

Extra forms

GENERAL JOURNAL

PAGE

	DATE	ACCOUNT TITLE	DOC. NO.	POST. REF.	DEBIT	CREDIT	
1							1
2							2
3							3
4							4
5							5
6							6
7							7
8							8
9							9
10							10

CASH PAYMENTS JOURNAL

PAGE

				1	2	3	4	5	
	DATE	ACCOUNT TITLE	CK. NO.	POST. REF.	GENERAL DEBIT	GENERAL CREDIT	ACCOUNTS PAYABLE DEBIT	PURCHASES DISCOUNT CREDIT	CASH CREDIT	
1										1
2										2
3										3
4										4
5										5
6										6
7										7
8										8
9										9
10										10

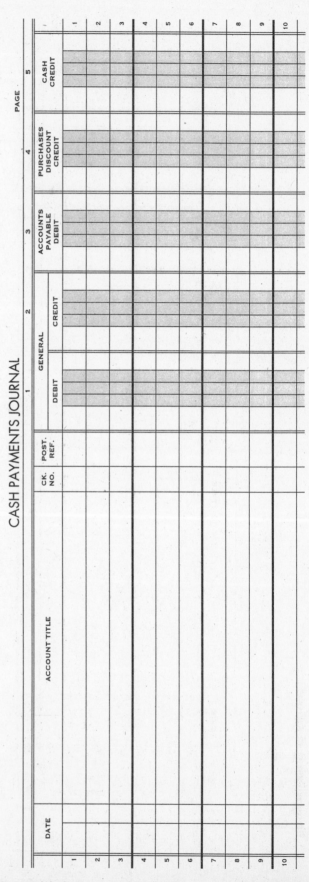

25-2 APPLICATION PROBLEM, p. 654

Journalizing dividends

1.

GENERAL JOURNAL

PAGE 12

DATE	ACCOUNT TITLE	DOC. NO.	POST. REF.	DEBIT	CREDIT

2.

CASH PAYMENTS JOURNAL

PAGE 18

DATE	ACCOUNT TITLE	CK. NO.	POST. REF.	GENERAL DEBIT	GENERAL CREDIT	ACCOUNTS PAYABLE DEBIT	PURCHASES DISCOUNT CREDIT	CASH CREDIT

GENERAL JOURNAL

DATE	ACCOUNT TITLE	DOC. NO.	POST. REF.	DEBIT	CREDIT
1						1
2						2
3						3
4						4
5						5
6						6
7						7
8						8
9						9

CASH PAYMENTS JOURNAL

DATE	ACCOUNT TITLE	CK. NO.	POST. REF.	GENERAL DEBIT	GENERAL CREDIT	ACCOUNTS PAYABLE DEBIT	PURCHASES DISCOUNT CREDIT	CASH CREDIT
1									1
2									2
3									3
4									4
5									5
6									6
7									7
8									8
9									9
10									10

Extra form

ACCOUNT TITLE	TRIAL BALANCE		ADJUSTMENTS		INCOME STATEMENT		BALANCE SHEET	
	1 DEBIT	2 CREDIT	3 DEBIT	4 CREDIT	5 DEBIT	6 CREDIT	7 DEBIT	8 CREDIT
29								
30								
31								
32								
33								
34								
35								
36								
37								
38								
39								
40								
41								
42								
43								
44								
45								
46								
47								
48								
49								
50								
51								
52								
53								
54								
55								
56								
57								

25-3 and 25-4 APPLICATION PROBLEMS, pp. 654, 655

25-3 Preparing a work sheet for a corporation
25-4 Completing a work sheet for a corporation

Donovan Lumber Corporation
Work Sheet
For Year Ended December 31, 20 – –

	ACCOUNT TITLE	TRIAL BALANCE DEBIT	TRIAL BALANCE CREDIT	ADJUSTMENTS DEBIT	ADJUSTMENTS CREDIT	INCOME STATEMENT DEBIT	INCOME STATEMENT CREDIT	BALANCE SHEET DEBIT	BALANCE SHEET CREDIT
1	Cash	2 8 4 8 58							
2	Petty Cash	3 0 0 00							
3	Notes Receivable	5 8 4 8 80							
4	Interest Receivable								
5	Accounts Receivable	58 1 8 7 80							
6	Allowance for Uncoll. Accts.		6 6 48						
7	Merchandise Inventory	79 8 5 8 00							
8	Supplies	4 9 8 7 70							
9	Prepaid Insurance	8 9 4 8 00							
10	Office Equipment	25 4 8 8 00							
11	Accum. Depr.—Office Equip.		7 4 8 8 00						
12	Store Equipment	18 4 9 8 00							
13	Accum. Depr.—Store Equip.		4 8 7 1 40						
14	Notes Payable		30 0 0 0 00						
15	Interest Payable								
16	Accounts Payable		8 4 7 2 80						
17	Employee Income Tax Pay.		1 4 8 6 30						
18	Federal Income Tax Payable								
19	Social Security Tax Payable		1 2 0 9 81						
20	Medicare Tax Payable		2 7 9 19						
21	Sales Tax Payable		2 8 4 7 00						
22	Unemploy. Tax Pay.—Fed.		2 9 25						
23	Unemploy. Tax Pay.—State		1 9 5 00						
24	Health Ins. Premiums Pay.		2 4 8 80						
25	Dividends Payable		5 0 0 0 00						
26	Capital Stock		50 0 0 0 00						
27	Retained Earnings		30 8 2 3 18						
28	Dividends	20 0 0 0 00							

25-3 and 25-4 APPLICATION PROBLEMS (concluded)

Donovan Lumber Corporation
Work Sheet (continued)
For Year Ended December 31, 20 - -

	ACCOUNT TITLE	TRIAL BALANCE DEBIT	TRIAL BALANCE CREDIT	ADJUSTMENTS DEBIT	ADJUSTMENTS CREDIT	INCOME STATEMENT DEBIT	INCOME STATEMENT CREDIT	BALANCE SHEET DEBIT	BALANCE SHEET CREDIT
29	Income Summary								
30	Sales		984 8 37 20						
31	Sales Discount	1 8 9 4 50							
32	Sales Ret. and Allowances	4 5 8 3 50							
33	Purchases	69 8 3 18 50							
34	Purchases Discount		4 2 1 5 50						
35	Purchases Ret. and Allow.		1 8 4 8 47						
36	Advertising Expense	8 4 8 3 80							
37	Cash Short and Over	1 0 20							
38	Credit Card Fee Expense	8 4 8 2 90							
39	Depr. Exp.—Office Equip.								
40	Depr. Exp.—Store Equip.								
41	Insurance Expense								
42	Miscellaneous Expense	9 1 8 4 80							
43	Payroll Taxes Expense	12 8 4 8 00							
44	Rent Expense	15 0 0 0 00							
45	Repair Expense	3 1 0 4 80							
46	Salary Expense	125 4 8 3 20							
47	Supplies Expense								
48	Uncollectible Accounts Exp.								
49	Utilities Expense	7 1 5 8 90							
50	Gain on Plant Assets		7 1 5 00						
51	Interest Income		2 2 7 00						
52	Interest Expense	3 1 5 8 40							
53	Loss on Plant Assets	1 8 4 00							
54	Federal Income Tax Expense	12 0 0 0 00							
55		1134 8 6 0 38	1134 8 6 0 38						
56	Net Inc. after Fed. Inc. Tax								
57									

2. Total of Income Statement Credit column _____

  Less total of Income Statement Debit column
    before federal income tax _____

  Equals Net Income before Federal Income Tax _____

Extra form

	ACCOUNT TITLE	TRIAL BALANCE		ADJUSTMENTS		INCOME STATEMENT		BALANCE SHEET	
		1 DEBIT	2 CREDIT	3 DEBIT	4 CREDIT	5 DEBIT	6 CREDIT	7 DEBIT	8 CREDIT

25-5 MASTERY PROBLEM, p. 655

Journalizing dividends and preparing a work sheet for a corporation

1.

GENERAL JOURNAL

PAGE 12

DATE	ACCOUNT TITLE	DOC. NO.	POST. REF.	DEBIT	CREDIT

2.

CASH PAYMENTS JOURNAL

PAGE 18

DATE	ACCOUNT TITLE	CK. NO.	POST. REF.	GENERAL DEBIT	GENERAL CREDIT	ACCOUNTS PAYABLE DEBIT	PURCHASES DISCOUNT CREDIT	CASH CREDIT

3., 4., 6.

Pennington Corporation
Work Sheet
For Year Ended December 31, 20 – –

	ACCOUNT TITLE	TRIAL BALANCE DEBIT	TRIAL BALANCE CREDIT	ADJUSTMENTS DEBIT	ADJUSTMENTS CREDIT	INCOME STATEMENT DEBIT	INCOME STATEMENT CREDIT	BALANCE SHEET DEBIT	BALANCE SHEET CREDIT
1	Cash	5 8 4 3 00							
2	Petty Cash	2 0 0 00							
3	Notes Receivable	3 8 4 8 00							
4	Interest Receivable								
5	Accounts Receivable	128 4 9 3 00							
6	Allowance for Uncoll. Accts.		8 8 20						
7	Merchandise Inventory	225 0 7 8 00							
8	Supplies	1 2 8 9 48							
9	Prepaid Insurance	8 9 4 8 00							
10	Office Equipment	34 8 2 0 50							
11	Accum. Depr.—Office Equip.		8 4 8 9 50						
12	Store Equipment	29 8 4 8 25							
13	Accum. Depr.—Store Equip.		7 1 9 0 50						
14	Notes Payable		30 0 0 0 00						
15	Interest Payable								
16	Accounts Payable		18 4 8 7 80						
17	Employee Income Tax Pay.		1 6 8 4 20						
18	Federal Income Tax Payable								
19	Social Security Tax Payable		1 1 2 5 27						
20	Medicare Tax Payable		2 5 9 68						
21	Sales Tax Payable		3 1 0 5 90						
22	Unemploy. Tax Pay.—Fed.		3 3 75						
23	Unemploy. Tax Pay.—State		2 2 5 00						
24	Health Ins. Premiums Pay.		3 1 8 40						
25	Dividends Payable		10 0 0 0 00						
26	Capital Stock		100 0 0 0 00						
27	Retained Earnings		70 3 8 7 26						
28	Dividends	40 0 0 0 00							

25-5 MASTERY PROBLEM (concluded)

3., 4., 6.

Pennington Corporation
Work Sheet (continued)
For Year Ended December 31, 20 – –

| | TRIAL BALANCE | | ADJUSTMENTS | | INCOME STATEMENT | | BALANCE SHEET | |
ACCOUNT TITLE	DEBIT	CREDIT	DEBIT	CREDIT	DEBIT	CREDIT	DEBIT	CREDIT
29 Income Summary								
30 Sales		1487831 08						
31 Sales Discount	2483 60							
32 Sales Ret. and Allowances	5310 40							
33 Purchases	948918 00							
34 Purchases Discount		6481 00						
35 Purchases Ret. and Allow.		12848 70						
36 Advertising Expense	15483 00							
37 Cash Short and Over	25 15							
38 Credit Card Fee Expense	9481 00							
39 Depr. Exp.—Office Equip.								
40 Depr. Exp.—Store Equip.								
41 Insurance Expense								
42 Miscellaneous Expense	15480 50							
43 Payroll Taxes Expense	13894 00							
44 Rent Expense	24000 00							
45 Repair Expense	3410 90							
46 Salary Expense	148384 74							
47 Supplies Expense								
48 Uncollectible Accounts Exp.								
49 Utilities Expense	8197 56							
50 Gain on Plant Assets		178 80						
51 Interest Income		348 60						
52 Interest Expense	4982 36							
53 Loss on Plant Assets	664 20							
54 Federal Income Tax Expense	80000 00							
55	1759083 64	1759 083 64						
56 Net Inc. after Fed. Inc. Tax								
57								

5. Total of Income Statement Credit column _____

   Less total of Income Statement Debit column
        before federal income tax   _____

   Equals Net Income before Federal Income Tax _____

Extra form

ACCOUNT TITLE		TRIAL BALANCE		ADJUSTMENTS		INCOME STATEMENT		BALANCE SHEET	
		DEBIT	CREDIT	DEBIT	CREDIT	DEBIT	CREDIT	DEBIT	CREDIT
	1								
	2								
	3								
	4								
	5								
	6								
	7								
	8								
	9								
	10								
	11								
	12								
	13								
	14								
	15								
	16								
	17								
	18								
	19								
	20								
	21								
	22								
	23								
	24								
	25								
	26								
	27								
	28								

25-6 CHALLENGE PROBLEM, p. 656

Completing a work sheet for a corporation

2.

Petal Corporation

Work Sheet

For Year Ended December 31, 20 – –

| | TRIAL BALANCE | | ADJUSTMENTS | | INCOME STATEMENT | | BALANCE SHEET | |
| | 1 | 2 | 3 | 4 | 5 | 6 | 7 | 8 |
ACCOUNT TITLE	DEBIT	CREDIT	DEBIT	CREDIT	DEBIT	CREDIT	DEBIT	CREDIT
18 Federal Income Tax Payable								
53 Loss on Plant Assets	4 5 6 00				4 5 6 00			
54 Federal Income Tax Expense	4 0 0 0 00							
55	4485 3 15 15	4485 3 15 15						
56 Net Inc. after Fed. Inc. Tax								
57								
58								
Column totals before income tax adjustment			75,543.21	75,543.21	2,852,510.25	2,994,267.03	1,648,964.97	1,547,208.19

1.

Total of Income Statement Credit column _____

Less total of Income Statement Debit column
before federal income tax _____

Equals Net Income before Federal Income Tax _____

2. _____

3.

Extra form

								% OF NET SALES

26-1 WORK TOGETHER, p. 665

Preparing an income statement for a corporation

Webster Corporation
Work Sheet
For Year Ended December 31, 20 – –

	Trial Balance		Adjustments		Income Statement		Balance Sheet	
Account Title	Debit	Credit	Debit	Credit	Debit	Credit	Debit	Credit
1. Cash	90 052 23						90 052 23	
2. Petty Cash	300 00						300 00	
3. Notes Receivable	10 952 00						10 952 00	
4. Interest Receivable			(a) 275 00				275 00	
5. Accounts Receivable	70 094 10						70 094 10	
6. Allowance for Uncoll. Accts.		44 64		(b) 7 350 00				7 394 64
7. Merchandise Inventory	64 316 30		(c) 25 800 00				90 116 30	
8. Supplies	2 552 08			(d) 2 300 00			252 08	
9. Prepaid Insurance	9 071 60			(e) 6 000 00			3 071 60	
10. Office Equipment	27 940 00						27 940 00	
11. Accum. Depr.—Office Equip.		6 735 00		(f) 2 800 00				9 535 00
12. Store Equipment	22 199 20						22 199 20	
13. Accum. Depr.—Store Equip.		6 357 40		(g) 1 700 60				8 058 00
14. Notes Payable		14 400 00						14 400 00
15. Interest Payable				(h) 555 16				555 16
16. Accounts Payable		60 116 18						60 116 18
17. Employee Inc. Tax Payable		1 652 40						1 652 40
18. Federal Inc. Tax Payable				(i) 1 752 70				1 752 70
19. Social Security Tax Payable		1 549 19						1 549 19
20. Medicare Tax Payable		357 51						357 51
21. Sales Tax Payable		6 652 60						6 652 60
22. Unemploy. Tax Pay.—Fed.		33 44						33 44
23. Unemploy. Tax Pay.—State		225 72						225 72
24. Health Ins. Premiums Pay.		702 60						702 60
25. Dividends Payable		10 800 00						10 800 00
26. Capital Stock		100 000 00						100 000 00
27. Retained Earnings		59 241 54						59 241 54
28. Dividends	43 200 00						43 200 00	
29. Income Summary				(c) 25 800 00		25 800 00		
30. Sales		1075 868 30				1075 868 30		
31. Sales Discount	2 020 80				2 020 80			
32. Sales Ret. and Allowances	8 347 20				8 347 20			

Webster Corporation

Work Sheet (continued)

For Year Ended December 31, 20 – –

	ACCOUNT TITLE	TRIAL BALANCE DEBIT	TRIAL BALANCE CREDIT	ADJUSTMENTS DEBIT	ADJUSTMENTS CREDIT	INCOME STATEMENT DEBIT	INCOME STATEMENT CREDIT	BALANCE SHEET DEBIT	BALANCE SHEET CREDIT
33	Purchases	737 464 80				737 464 80			
34	Purchases Discount		5 483 60				5 483 60		
35	Purchases Ret. and Allow.		2 716 14				2 716 14		
36	Advertising Expense	15 947 00				15 947 00			
37	Cash Short and Over	9 15				9 15			
38	Credit Card Fee Expense	10 066 94				10 066 94			
39	Depr. Exp.—Office Equip.			(e) 2 800 00		2 800 00			
40	Depr. Exp.—Store Equip.			(f) 1 700 60		1 700 60			
41	Insurance Expense			(g) 6 000 00		6 000 00			
42	Miscellaneous Expense	8 682 20				8 682 20			
43	Payroll Taxes Expense	14 966 00				14 966 00			
44	Rent Expense	28 915 00				28 915 00			
45	Repair Expense	3 485 00				3 485 00			
46	Salary Expense	158 964 00				158 964 00			
47	Supplies Expense			(d) 2 300 00		2 300 00			
48	Uncollectible Accounts Exp.			(b) 7 350 00		7 350 00			
49	Utilities Expense	2 661 00				2 661 00			
50	Gain on Plant Assets		1 100 00				1 100 00		
51	Interest Income		894 48		(a) 275 00		1 169 48		
52	Interest Expense	2 186 14		(h) 555 16		2 741 30			
53	Loss on Plant Assets	2 480 00				2 480 00			
54	Federal Income Tax Expense	19 300 00		(i) 1 752 70		21 052 70			
55		1353 940 74	1353 940 74	48 533 46	48 533 46	1035 721 69	1111 147 52	358 452 51	283 026 68
56	Net Inc. after Fed. Inc. Tax					75 425 83			75 425 83
57						1111 147 52	1111 147 52	358 452 51	358 452 51
58									
59									
60									
61									
62									

(Note: This Work Together continues on page 272.)

Preparing an income statement for a corporation

Osborn Corporation
Work Sheet
For Year Ended December 31, 20 – –

#	ACCOUNT TITLE	TRIAL BALANCE DEBIT	TRIAL BALANCE CREDIT	ADJUSTMENTS DEBIT	ADJUSTMENTS CREDIT	INCOME STATEMENT DEBIT	INCOME STATEMENT CREDIT	BALANCE SHEET DEBIT	BALANCE SHEET CREDIT
1	Cash	7848 00						7848 00	
2	Petty Cash	250 00						250 00	
3	Notes Receivable	11954 00						11954 00	
4	Interest Receivable			(a) 545 20				545 20	
5	Accounts Receivable	75171 69						75171 69	
6	Allowance for Uncoll. Accts.		80 53		(b) 13000 00				13080 53
7	Merchandise Inventory	88548 50		(c)16048 56				104597 06	
8	Supplies	4835 80			(d) 3739 27			1096 53	
9	Prepaid Insurance	12518 00			(e) 6148 00			6370 00	
10	Office Equipment	36184 00						36184 00	
11	Accum. Depr.—Office Equip.		8478 00		(f) 5500 00				13978 00
12	Store Equipment	30184 50						30184 50	
13	Accum. Depr.—Store Equip.		11848 50		(g) 6800 00				18648 50
14	Notes Payable		20000 00						20000 00
15	Interest Payable				(h) 500 00				500 00
16	Accounts Payable		24718 80						24718 80
17	Employee Inc. Tax Payable		1584 50						1584 50
18	Federal Inc. Tax Payable				(i) 741 47				741 47
19	Social Security Tax Payable		1487 20						1487 20
20	Medicare Tax Payable		343 20						343 20
21	Sales Tax Payable		5848 20						5848 20
22	Unemploy. Tax Pay.—Fed.		30 87						30 87
23	Unemploy. Tax Pay.—State		205 80						205 80
24	Health Ins. Premiums Pay.		702 60						702 60
25	Dividends Payable		15000 00						15000 00
26	Capital Stock		80000 00						80000 00
27	Retained Earnings		56106 89						56106 89
28	Dividends	25000 00						25000 00	
29	Income Summary				(c)16048 56		16048 56		
30	Sales		1183835 00				1183835 00		
31	Sales Discount	2318 80				2318 80			
32	Sales Ret. and Allowances	8105 50				8105 50			

26-1 ON YOUR OWN (continued)

Osborn Corporation

Work Sheet (continued)

For Year Ended December 31, 20 --

	Account Title	Trial Balance Debit	Trial Balance Credit	Adjustments Debit	Adjustments Credit	Income Statement Debit	Income Statement Credit	Balance Sheet Debit	Balance Sheet Credit
33	Purchases	857789 20				857789 20			
34	Purchases Discount		6154 80				6154 80		
35	Purchases Ret. and Allow.		2218 80				2218 80		
36	Advertising Expense	168484 20				168484 20			
37	Cash Short and Over	12 50				12 50			
38	Credit Card Fee Expense	12486 90				12486 90			
39	Depr. Exp.—Office Equip.			(c) 5500 00		5500 00			
40	Depr. Exp.—Store Equip.			(g) 6800 00		6800 00			
41	Insurance Expense			(e) 6148 00		6148 00			
42	Miscellaneous Expense	9789 00				9789 00			
43	Payroll Taxes Expense	15483 00				15483 00			
44	Rent Expense	19700 00				19700 00			
45	Repair Expense	4848 80				4848 80			
46	Salary Expense	160318 50				160318 50			
47	Supplies Expense			(d) 3739 27		3739 27			
48	Uncollectible Accounts Exp.			(b) 13000 00		13000 00			
49	Utilities Expense	8153 80				8153 80			
50	Gain on Plant Assets		514 00				514 00		
51	Interest Income		158 00		(a) 545 20		703 20		
52	Interest Expense	2639 00		(h) 500 00		3139 00			
53	Loss on Plant Assets	328 00				328 00			
54	Federal Income Tax Expense	8000 00		(i) 741 47		8741 47			
55		1419 3 15 69	1419 3 15 69	53 02 25 0	53 02 25 0	1163 2 4 99	1209 4 7 36	299 2 00 98	252 9 7 56
56	Net Inc. after Fed. Inc. Tax					46 2 2 42			46 2 2 42
57						1209 4 7 36	1209 4 7 36	299 2 00 98	299 2 00 98
58									
59									
60									
61									
62									

(Note: This On Your Own continues on page 274.)

4.

					% OF NET SALES

26-1 WORK TOGETHER (concluded)

4.

		% OF NET SALES

5.

	Acceptable %	Actual %	Positive Result		Recommended Action If Needed
			Yes	No	
Cost of merchandise sold	Not more than 68.0%				
Gross profit on operations	Not less than 32.0%				
Total operating expenses	Not more than 22.0%				
Income from operations	Not less than 10.0%				
Net deduction from other revenue and expenses	Not more than 0.1%				
Net income before federal income tax	Not less than 9.8%				

6.

									% OF NET SALES

26-1 ON YOUR OWN (concluded)

6.

					% OF NET SALES

7.

	Acceptable %	Actual %	Positive Result		Recommended Action If Needed
			Yes	No	
Cost of merchandise sold	Not more than 70.0%				
Gross profit on operations	Not less than 30.0%				
Total operating expenses	Not more than 25.0%				
Income from operations	Not less than 5.0%				
Net deduction from other revenue and expenses	Not more than 0.1%				
Net income before federal income tax	Not less than 4.9%				

Extra form

											% OF NET SALES

26-2 WORK TOGETHER, p. 668

Preparing a statement of stockholders' equity for a corporation

Preparing a statement of stockholders' equity for a corporation

26-3 WORK TOGETHER, p. 674

Preparing and analyzing a balance sheet for a corporation

7.

26-3 WORK TOGETHER (concluded)

7.

8., 9.

	Acceptable	Actual	Positive Result		Recommended Action If Needed
			Yes	No	
Working capital	Not less than $150,000				
Current ratio	Between 2.0 to 1 and 3.0 to 1				

Preparing and analyzing a balance sheet for a corporation

10.

26-3 **ON YOUR OWN (concluded)**

10.

11., 12.

	Acceptable	Actual	Positive Result		Recommended Action If Needed
			Yes	No	
Working capital	Not less than $100,000				
Current ratio	Between 2.0 to 1 and 3.0 to 1				

Extra form

26-4 WORK TOGETHER, p. 681

Journalizing adjusting, closing, and reversing entries for a corporation

4.

GENERAL JOURNAL   PAGE 15

	DATE	ACCOUNT TITLE	DOC. NO.	POST. REF.	DEBIT	CREDIT	
1							1
2							2
3							3
4							4
5							5
6							6
7							7
8							8
9							9
10							10
11							11
12							12
13							13
14							14
15							15
16							16
17							17
18							18
19							19
20							20
21							21
22							22
23							23
24							24
25							25
26							26
27							27
28							28
29							29
30							30
31							31
32							32

5.

GENERAL JOURNAL

	DATE	ACCOUNT TITLE	DOC. NO.	POST. REF.	DEBIT	CREDIT	
1							1
2							2
3							3
4							4
5							5
6							6
7							7
8							8
9							9
10							10
11							11
12							12
13							13
14							14
15							15
16							16
17							17
18							18
19							19
20							20
21							21
22							22
23							23
24							24
25							25
26							26
27							27
28							28
29							29
30							30
31							31
32							32
33							33

26-4 **WORK TOGETHER (concluded)**

6.

GENERAL JOURNAL   PAGE 17

	DATE		ACCOUNT TITLE	DOC. NO.	POST. REF.	DEBIT	CREDIT	
1								1
2								2
3								3
4								4
5								5
6								6
7								7
8								8
9								9
10								10
11								11
12								12
13								13
14								14
15								15
16								16
17								17
18								18
19								19
20								20
21								21
22								22
23								23
24								24
25								25
26								26
27								27
28								28
29								29
30								30
31								31
32								32
33								33

Journalizing adjusting, closing, and reversing entries for a corporation

7.

GENERAL JOURNAL

	DATE		ACCOUNT TITLE	DOC. NO.	POST. REF.	DEBIT	CREDIT	
1								1
2								2
3								3
4								4
5								5
6								6
7								7
8								8
9								9
10								10
11								11
12								12
13								13
14								14
15								15
16								16
17								17
18								18
19								19
20								20
21								21
22								22
23								23
24								24
25								25
26								26
27								27
28								28
29								29
30								30
31								31
32								32

26-4 **ON YOUR OWN (continued)**

8.

GENERAL JOURNAL

	DATE		ACCOUNT TITLE	DOC. NO.	POST. REF.	DEBIT	CREDIT	
1								1
2								2
3								3
4								4
5								5
6								6
7								7
8								8
9								9
10								10
11								11
12								12
13								13
14								14
15								15
16								16
17								17
18								18
19								19
20								20
21								21
22								22
23								23
24								24
25								25
26								26
27								27
28								28
29								29
30								30
31								31
32								32
33								33

9.

GENERAL JOURNAL   PAGE 20

	DATE		ACCOUNT TITLE	DOC. NO.	POST. REF.	DEBIT	CREDIT	
1								1
2								2
3								3
4								4
5								5
6								6
7								7
8								8
9								9
10								10
11								11
12								12
13								13
14								14
15								15
16								16
17								17
18								18
19								19
20								20
21								21
22								22
23								23
24								24
25								25
26								26
27								27
28								28
29								29
30								30
31								31
32								32
33								33

26-1 APPLICATION PROBLEM, p. 683

Preparing an income statement for a corporation

Donovan Lumber Corporation
Work Sheet
For Year Ended December 31, 20 - -

ACCOUNT TITLE	TRIAL BALANCE DEBIT	TRIAL BALANCE CREDIT	ADJUSTMENTS DEBIT	ADJUSTMENTS CREDIT	INCOME STATEMENT DEBIT	INCOME STATEMENT CREDIT	BALANCE SHEET DEBIT	BALANCE SHEET CREDIT
1 Cash	3 848 58						3 848 58	
2 Petty Cash	300 00						300 00	
3 Notes Receivable	5 848 80						5 848 80	
4 Interest Receivable			(a) 315 00				315 00	
5 Accounts Receivable	57 187 80						57 187 80	
6 Allowance for Uncoll. Accts.		66 48		(b) 6 850 00				6 916 48
7 Merchandise Inventory	78 858 00		2 426 50				81 284 50	
8 Supplies	4 987 70			(d) 3 140 20			1 847 50	
9 Prepaid Insurance	8 948 00			(e) 4 768 00			4 180 00	
10 Office Equipment	26 488 00						26 488 00	
11 Accum. Depr.—Office Equip.		8 488 00		(f) 3 128 00				11 616 00
12 Store Equipment	17 498 00						17 498 00	
13 Accum. Depr.—Store Equip.		4 871 40		(g) 3 389 00				8 260 40
14 Notes Payable		30 000 00						30 000 00
15 Interest Payable				(h) 300 00				300 00
16 Accounts Payable		8 372 80						8 372 80
17 Employee Inc. Tax Payable		1 486 30						1 486 30
18 Federal Inc. Tax Payable				(i) 1 278 49				1 278 49
19 Social Security Tax Payable		1 209 81						1 209 81
20 Medicare Tax Payable		279 19						279 19
21 Sales Tax Payable		2 847 00						2 847 00
22 Unemploy. Tax Pay.—Fed.		29 25						29 25
23 Unemploy. Tax Pay.—State		195 00						195 00
24 Health Ins. Premiums Pay.		348 80						348 80
25 Dividends Payable		5 000 00						5 000 00
26 Capital Stock		50 000 00						50 000 00
27 Retained Earnings		30 823 18						30 823 18
28 Dividends	20 000 00						20 000 00	
29 Income Summary				(c) 2 426 50		2 426 50		
30 Sales		983 837 20				983 837 20		
31 Sales Discount	1 894 50				1 894 50			
32 Sales Ret. and Allowances	4 583 50				4 583 50			

Donovan Lumber Corporation
Work Sheet (continued)
For Year Ended December 31, 20--

	Account Title	Trial Balance Debit	Trial Balance Credit	Adjustments Debit	Adjustments Credit	Income Statement Debit	Income Statement Credit	Balance Sheet Debit	Balance Sheet Credit
33	Purchases	697318 50				697318 50			
34	Purchases Discount		4215 50				4215 50		
35	Purchases Ret. and Allow.		1848 47				1848 47		
36	Advertising Expense	9483 80				9483 80			
37	Cash Short and Over	10 20				10 20			
38	Credit Card Fee Expense	8482 90				8482 90			
39	Depr. Exp.—Office Equip.			(c) 3128 00		3128 00			
40	Depr. Exp.—Store Equip.			(d) 3389 00		3389 00			
41	Insurance Expense			(e) 4768 00		4768 00			
42	Miscellaneous Expense	9184 80				9184 80			
43	Payroll Taxes Expense	12848 00				12848 00			
44	Rent Expense	15000 00				15000 00			
45	Repair Expense	4104 80				4104 80			
46	Salary Expense	125483 20				125483 20			
47	Supplies Expense			(d) 3140 20		3140 20			
48	Uncollectible Accounts Exp.			(e) 6850 00		6850 00			
49	Utilities Expense	7158 90				7158 90			
50	Gain on Plant Assets		7150 00				7150 00		
51	Interest Income		227 00		(a) 315 00		542 00		
52	Interest Expense	3158 40		300 00		3458 40			
53	Loss on Plant Assets	184 00				184 00			
54	Federal Income Tax Expense	12000 00		(f) 1278 49		13278 49			
55		1134 860 38	1134 860 38	25595 19	25595 19	933749 19	993584 67	218798 18	158962 70
56	Net Inc. after Fed. Inc. Tax					59835 48			59835 48
57						993584 67	993584 67	218798 18	218798 18

Extra form

												% OF NET SALES

26-1 APPLICATION PROBLEM (continued)

1., 2.

							% OF NET SALES

26-1 APPLICATION PROBLEM (concluded)

1., 2.

									% OF NET SALES

3.

	Acceptable %	Actual %	Positive Result		Recommended Action If Needed
			Yes	No	
Cost of merchandise sold	Not more than 70.0%				
Gross profit on operations	Not less than 30.0%				
Total operating expenses	Not more than 25.0%				
Income from operations	Not less than 5.0%				
Net deduction from other revenue and expenses	Not more than 0.1%				
Net income before federal income tax	Not less than 4.9%				

Extra form

										% OF NET SALES

26-2 APPLICATION PROBLEM, p. 683

Preparing a statement of stockholders' equity for a corporation

Extra form

Extra form

26-3 APPLICATION PROBLEM, p. 683

1. Preparing and analyzing a balance sheet for a corporation

26-3 APPLICATION PROBLEM (concluded)

1.

(blank accounting form with multiple amount columns)

2.

	Acceptable	Actual	Positive Result		Recommended Action If Needed
			Yes	No	
Working capital	Not less than $100,000				
Current ratio	Between 3.0 to 1 and 3.5 to 1				

Extra form

26-4 APPLICATION PROBLEM, p. 684

Journalizing adjusting, closing, and reversing entries for a corporation

1.

GENERAL JOURNAL

	DATE	ACCOUNT TITLE	DOC. NO.	POST. REF.	DEBIT	CREDIT	
1							1
2							2
3							3
4							4
5							5
6							6
7							7
8							8
9							9
10							10
11							11
12							12
13							13
14							14
15							15
16							16
17							17
18							18
19							19
20							20
21							21
22							22
23							23
24							24
25							25
26							26
27							27
28							28
29							29
30							30
31							31
32							32

2.

GENERAL JOURNAL

	DATE		ACCOUNT TITLE	DOC. NO.	POST. REF.	DEBIT	CREDIT	
1								1
2								2
3								3
4								4
5								5
6								6
7								7
8								8
9								9
10								10
11								11
12								12
13								13
14								14
15								15
16								16
17								17
18								18
19								19
20								20
21								21
22								22
23								23
24								24
25								25
26								26
27								27
28								28
29								29
30								30
31								31
32								32
33								33

26-4 APPLICATION PROBLEM (concluded)

3.

GENERAL JOURNAL

	DATE	ACCOUNT TITLE	DOC. NO.	POST. REF.	DEBIT	CREDIT	
1							1
2							2
3							3
4							4
5							5
6							6
7							7
8							8
9							9
10							10
11							11
12							12
13							13
14							14
15							15
16							16
17							17
18							18
19							19
20							20
21							21
22							22
23							23
24							24
25							25
26							26
27							27
28							28
29							29
30							30
31							31
32							32
33							33

Extra form

GENERAL JOURNAL

	DATE	ACCOUNT TITLE	DOC. NO.	POST. REF.	DEBIT	CREDIT	
1							1
2							2
3							3
4							4
5							5
6							6
7							7
8							8
9							9
10							10
11							11
12							12
13							13
14							14
15							15
16							16
17							17
18							18
19							19
20							20
21							21
22							22
23							23
24							24
25							25
26							26
27							27
28							28
29							29
30							30
31							31
32							32
33							33

26-5 MASTERY PROBLEM, p. 684

Preparing financial statements and end-of-fiscal-period entries for a corporation

Pennington Corporation
Work Sheet
For Year Ended December 31, 20 — —

Account Title	Trial Balance Debit	Trial Balance Credit	Adjustments Debit	Adjustments Credit	Income Statement Debit	Income Statement Credit	Balance Sheet Debit	Balance Sheet Credit
1 Cash	6843 00						6843 00	
2 Petty Cash	200 00						200 00	
3 Notes Receivable	3848 00						3848 00	
4 Interest Receivable			(a) 685 00				685 00	
5 Accounts Receivable	127493 00						127493 00	
6 Allowance for Uncoll. Accts.		88 20		(b) 9570 00				9658 20
7 Merchandise Inventory	226078 00			(c) 6490 80			219587 20	
8 Supplies	1289 48			(d) 958 08			331 40	
9 Prepaid Insurance	8948 00			(e) 4848 00			4100 00	
10 Office Equipment	35820 50						35820 50	
11 Accum. Depr.—Office Equip.		8489 50		(f) 5747 00				14236 50
12 Store Equipment	28848 25						28848 25	
13 Accum. Depr.—Store Equip.		7190 50		(g) 4510 00				11700 50
14 Notes Payable		30000 00						30000 00
15 Interest Payable				(h) 400 00				400 00
16 Accounts Payable		18987 80						18987 80
17 Employee Inc. Tax Payable		1684 20						1684 20
18 Federal Inc. Tax Payable				(i) 10747 22				10747 22
19 Social Security Tax Payable		1125 27						1125 27
20 Medicare Tax Payable		259 68						259 68
21 Sales Tax Payable		3105 90						3105 90
22 Unemploy. Tax Pay.—Fed.		33 75						33 75
23 Unemploy. Tax Pay.—State		225 00						225 00
24 Health Ins. Premiums Pay.		318 40						318 40
25 Dividends Payable		10000 00						10000 00
26 Capital Stock		100000 00						100000 00
27 Retained Earnings		70387 26						70387 26
28 Dividends	40000 00						40000 00	
29 Income Summary			(c) 6490 80		6490 80			
30 Sales		1486831 08				1486831 08		
31 Sales Discount	2483 60				2483 60			
32 Sales Ret. and Allowances	5310 40				5310 40			

Pennington Corporation
Work Sheet (continued)
For Year Ended December 31, 20 – –

#	Account Title	Trial Balance Debit	Trial Balance Credit	Adjustments Debit	Adjustments Credit	Income Statement Debit	Income Statement Credit	Balance Sheet Debit	Balance Sheet Credit
33	Purchases	947918 00				947918 00			
34	Purchases Discount		6481 00				6481 00		
35	Purchases Ret. and Allow.		12848 70				12848 70		
36	Advertising Expense	14483 00				14483 00			
37	Cash Short and Over	25 15				25 15			
38	Credit Card Fee Expense	9481 00				9481 00			
39	Depr. Exp.—Office Equip.			(f) 5747 00		5747 00			
40	Depr. Exp.—Store Equip.			(g) 4510 00		4510 00			
41	Insurance Expense			(e) 4848 00		4848 00			
42	Miscellaneous Expense	14780 50				14780 50			
43	Payroll Taxes Expense	13894 00				13894 00			
44	Rent Expense	24000 00				24000 00			
45	Repair Expense	3410 90				3410 90			
46	Salary Expense	148384 74				148384 74			
47	Supplies Expense			(d) 958 08		958 08			
48	Uncollectible Accounts Exp.			(b) 9570 00		9570 00			
49	Utilities Expense	10197 56				10197 56			
50	Gain on Plant Assets		178 80				178 80		
51	Interest Income		348 60		(c) 685 00		1033 60		
52	Interest Expense	4182 36		(h) 400 00		4582 36			
53	Loss on Plant Assets	6646 20				6646 20			
54	Federal Income Tax Expense	80000 00		(a) 10747 22		90747 22			
55		1758583 64	1758583 64	43956 10	43956 10	1322486 51	1507373 18	467756 35	282869 68
56	Net Inc. after Fed. Inc. Tax					184886 67			184886 67
57						1507373 18	1507373 18	467756 35	467756 35

Extra form

												% OF NET SALES

26-5 **MASTERY PROBLEM** (continued)

1.

								% OF NET SALES

26-5 **MASTERY PROBLEM (continued)**

1.

											% OF NET SALES

3.

4.

26-5 MASTERY PROBLEM (continued)

4. _____

_____

2. Income Statement Analysis

	Acceptable %	Actual %	Positive Result Yes	Positive Result No	Recommended Action If Needed
Cost of merchandise sold	Not more than 65.0%				
Gross profit on operations	Not less than 35.0%				
Total operating expenses	Not more than 16.0%				
Income from operations	Not less than 19.0%				
Net deduction from other revenue and expenses	Not more than 0.5%				
Net income before federal income tax	Not less than 18.5%				

5. Balance Sheet Analysis

	Acceptable	Actual	Positive Result Yes	Positive Result No	Recommended Action If Needed
Working capital	Not less than $150,000				
Current ratio	Between 3.0 to 1 and 4.0 to 1				

6.

GENERAL JOURNAL PAGE 15

	DATE	ACCOUNT TITLE	DOC. NO.	POST. REF.	DEBIT	CREDIT	
1							1
2							2
3							3
4							4
5							5
6							6
7							7
8							8
9							9
10							10
11							11
12							12
13							13
14							14
15							15
16							16
17							17
18							18
19							19
20							20
21							21
22							22
23							23
24							24
25							25
26							26
27							27
28							28
29							29
30							30
31							31
32							32
33							33

26-5 MASTERY PROBLEM (continued)

7.

GENERAL JOURNAL   PAGE 16

	DATE		ACCOUNT TITLE	DOC. NO.	POST. REF.	DEBIT	CREDIT	
1								1
2								2
3								3
4								4
5								5
6								6
7								7
8								8
9								9
10								10
11								11
12								12
13								13
14								14
15								15
16								16
17								17
18								18
19								19
20								20
21								21
22								22
23								23
24								24
25								25
26								26
27								27
28								28
29								29
30								30
31								31
32								32
33								33

8.

GENERAL JOURNAL

	DATE	ACCOUNT TITLE	DOC. NO.	POST. REF.	DEBIT	CREDIT	
1							1
2							2
3							3
4							4
5							5
6							6
7							7
8							8
9							9
10							10
11							11
12							12
13							13
14							14
15							15
16							16
17							17
18							18
19							19
20							20
21							21
22							22
23							23
24							24
25							25
26							26
27							27
28							28
29							29
30							30
31							31
32							32
33							33

26-6 CHALLENGE PROBLEM, p. 685

Analyzing financial strength

1.

Name of Corporation	Working Capital	Current Ratio
1.		
2.		

Calculations:

_____

_____

_____

_____

_____

_____

_____

_____

_____

_____

_____

_____

_____

_____

_____

2.

Extra form

	ACCOUNT TITLE	TRIAL BALANCE		ADJUSTMENTS		INCOME STATEMENT		BALANCE SHEET	
		DEBIT 1	CREDIT 2	DEBIT 3	CREDIT 4	DEBIT 5	CREDIT 6	DEBIT 7	CREDIT 8
29									
30									
31									
32									
33									
34									
35									
36									
37									
38									
39									
40									
41									
42									
43									
44									
45									
46									
47									
48									
49									
50									
51									
52									
53									
54									
55									
56									
57									

REINFORCEMENT ACTIVITY 3   PART B, p. 688

An Accounting Cycle for a Corporation: End-of-Fiscal-Period Work

The general ledger used in Reinforcement Activity 3, Part A, is needed to complete Part B.

12.

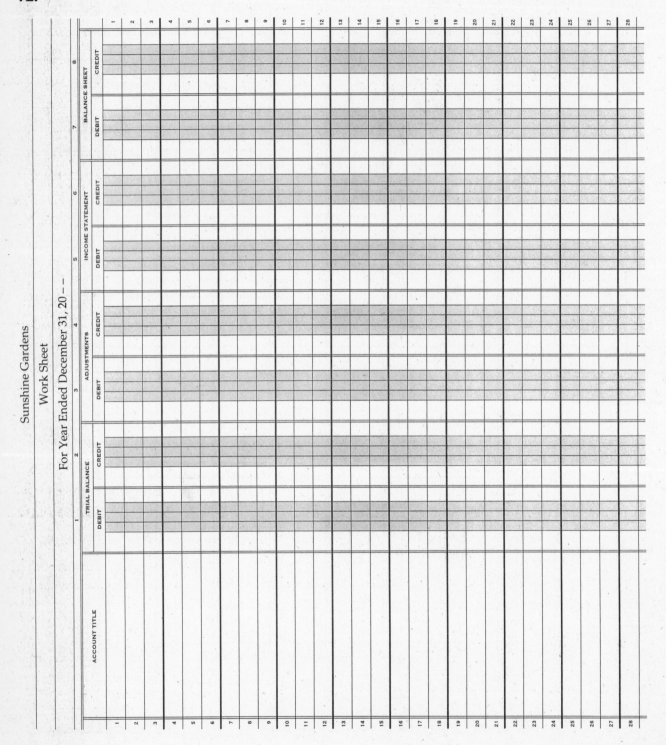

Sunshine Gardens
Work Sheet
For Year Ended December 31, 20 – –

REINFORCEMENT ACTIVITY 3 PART B (continued)

12.

Sunshine Gardens
Work Sheet (continued)
For Year Ended December 31, 20 - -

ACCOUNT TITLE	TRIAL BALANCE		ADJUSTMENTS		INCOME STATEMENT		BALANCE SHEET	
	DEBIT	CREDIT	DEBIT	CREDIT	DEBIT	CREDIT	DEBIT	CREDIT
	1	2	3	4	5	6	7	8

Extra form

	ACCOUNT TITLE		TRIAL BALANCE		ADJUSTMENTS		INCOME STATEMENT		BALANCE SHEET	
			DEBIT 1	CREDIT 2	DEBIT 3	CREDIT 4	DEBIT 5	CREDIT 6	DEBIT 7	CREDIT 8

Extra form

													% OF NET SALES

REINFORCEMENT ACTIVITY 3 **PART B (continued)**

13.

Sunshine Gardens

Income Statement

For the Year Ended December 31, 20 – –

				% OF NET SALES

REINFORCEMENT ACTIVITY 3 **PART B (continued)**

13.

Sunshine Gardens

Income Statement (continued)

For Year Ended December 31, 20 – –

				% OF NET SALES

15.

Sunshine Gardens

Statement of Stockholders' Equity

For Year Ended December 31, 20 – –

16.

Sunshine Gardens

Balance Sheet

December 31, 20 – –

REINFORCEMENT ACTIVITY 3 PART B (continued)

16.

Sunshine Gardens

Balance Sheet (continued)

December 31, 20 – –

14. Income Statement Analysis

	Acceptable %	Actual %	Positive Result		Recommended Action If Needed
			Yes	No	
Cost of merchandise sold	Not more than 62.0%				
Gross profit on operations	Not less than 38.0%				
Total operating expenses	Not more than 25.0%				
Income from operations	Not less than 13.0%				
Net deductions from other revenue and expenses	Not more than 0.5%				
Net income before federal income tax	Not less than 12.5%				

17. Balance Sheet Analysis

	Acceptable	Actual	Positive Result		Recommended Action If Needed
			Yes	No	
Working capital	Not less than $50,000.00				
Current ratio	Between 2.0 to 1 and 3.0 to 1				

18.

GENERAL JOURNAL   PAGE 13

	DATE		ACCOUNT TITLE	DOC. NO.	POST. REF.	DEBIT	CREDIT	
1								1
2								2
3								3
4								4
5								5
6								6
7								7
8								8
9								9
10								10
11								11
12								12
13								13
14								14
15								15
16								16
17								17
18								18
19								19
20								20
21								21
22								22
23								23
24								24
25								25
26								26
27								27
28								28
29								29
30								30
31								31
32								32
33								33

REINFORCEMENT ACTIVITY 3 **PART B (continued)**

19.

GENERAL JOURNAL   PAGE 14

	DATE	ACCOUNT TITLE	DOC. NO.	POST. REF.	DEBIT	CREDIT	
1							1
2							2
3							3
4							4
5							5
6							6
7							7
8							8
9							9
10							10
11							11
12							12
13							13
14							14
15							15
16							16
17							17
18							18
19							19
20							20
21							21
22							22
23							23
24							24
25							25
26							26
27							27
28							28
29							29
30							30
31							31
32							32
33							33

20.

Sunshine Gardens

Post-Closing Trial Balance

For Year Ended December 31, 20 – –

ACCOUNT TITLE	DEBIT	CREDIT

REINFORCEMENT ACTIVITY 3 **PART B (concluded)**

21.

GENERAL JOURNAL

	DATE		ACCOUNT TITLE	DOC. NO.	POST. REF.	DEBIT	CREDIT	
1								1
2								2
3								3
4								4
5								5
6								6
7								7
8								8
9								9
10								10
11								11
12								12
13								13
14								14
15								15
16								16
17								17
18								18
19								19
20								20
21								21
22								22
23								23
24								24
25								25
26								26
27								27
28								28
29								29
30								30
31								31
32								32
33								33

Extra form

GENERAL JOURNAL

PAGE _____

	DATE		ACCOUNT TITLE	DOC. NO.	POST. REF.	DEBIT	CREDIT	
1								1
2								2
3								3
4								4
5								5
6								6
7								7
8								8
9								9
10								10
11								11
12								12
13								13
14								14
15								15
16								16
17								17
18								18
19								19
20								20
21								21
22								22
23								23
24								24
25								25
26								26
27								27
28								28
29								29
30								30
31								31
32								32
33								33

Extra form

GENERAL JOURNAL   PAGE

	DATE		ACCOUNT TITLE	DOC. NO.	POST. REF.	DEBIT	CREDIT	
1								1
2								2
3								3
4								4
5								5
6								6
7								7
8								8
9								9
10								10
11								11
12								12
13								13
14								14
15								15
16								16
17								17
18								18
19								19
20								20
21								21
22								22
23								23
24								24
25								25
26								26
27								27
28								28
29								29
30								30
31								31
32								32
33								33

Extra form

Extra form

CASH RECEIPTS JOURNAL

PAGE

	DATE	ACCOUNT TITLE	DOC. NO.	POST. REF.	GENERAL DEBIT	GENERAL CREDIT	ACCOUNTS RECEIVABLE CREDIT	SALES CREDIT	SALES TAX PAYABLE DEBIT	SALES TAX PAYABLE CREDIT	SALES DISCOUNT DEBIT	CASH DEBIT	
					1	2	3	4	5	6	7	8	
1													1
2													2
3													3
4													4
5													5
6													6
7													7
8													8
9													9
10													10
11													11
12													12
13													13
14													14
15													15
16													16
17													17
18													18
19													19
20													20
21													21
22													22
23													23
24													24
25													25

Extra form

CASH PAYMENTS JOURNAL

PAGE

	DATE	ACCOUNT TITLE	CK. NO.	POST. REF.	GENERAL DEBIT	GENERAL CREDIT	ACCOUNTS PAYABLE DEBIT	PURCHASES DISCOUNT CREDIT	CASH CREDIT
1									
2									
3									
4									
5									
6									
7									
8									
9									
10									
11									
12									
13									
14									
15									
16									
17									
18									
19									
20									
21									
22									
23									
24									